External Scars from Internal Wounds

CINDY HYDE

Holman Christian Standard Bible®, Copyright © 1999, 2000, 2002, 2003, 2009 by Holman Bible Publishers.

Scripture taken from *The Message*. Copyright © 1993, 1994, 1995, 1996, 2000, 2001, 2002. Used by permission of NavPress Publishing Group

THE HOLY BIBLE, NEW INTERNATIONAL VERSION®, NIV® Copyright © 1973, 1978, 1984, 2011 by Biblica, Inc.® Used by permission. All rights reserved worldwide.

The Voice Bible Copyright © 2012 Thomas Nelson, Inc. The Voice™ translation © 2012 Ecclesia Bible Society All rights reserved.

ISBN-13: 978-1514685624
ISBN-10: 1514685620

DEDICATION

I dedicate this book to my son Shawn Paul Mixon and to everyone else who now has external scars from their internal wounds.

May each of you find peace and healing. May you find purpose and meaning for your life. May you find your path and fulfill your destiny. May your life become enjoyable and overflowing with goodness. May your purpose become evident to you so you can realize what a special and unique person you truly are.

CONTENTS

ACKNOWLEDGMENTS

I wish to personally thank and acknowledge the following people for their prayerful contributions to my life and this book, for being my friend, mentor, and helper. Each of you inspire me. Because of that… this project is a reality.

Jesus Christ and thank Him for the gift of life and for healing. My son, Shawn Paul Mixon, who inspired this book. Everyone who prayed for this project and my patient and understanding husband Michael Hyde… thank you. My friend Dr. John Handley, Ph.D., my mentors in the early years: Margie McMullen and Joan Buchanan, my sweet and prayerful friend Lucy Richardson, Kimberly Russell, Patty Gray, Edie & Darryl Bayer for believing in me and encouraging me, and my friends Richard Quick, Pastor Stanford Pensulo in Malawi, Pastor Samsoon Masih at the Pakistan Healing Center, Pastor Peter Tuito Gunn in East Kenya for their faithful prayers. And a special acknowledgement to all the anonymous authors in this book.

FORWARD

There is no "you" apart from your actual life. You are not separate from your life, and in that life you must find the goodness of God. Otherwise, you will not believe that he has done well by you, and you will not truly be at peace with him.

Dallas Willard
The Divine Conspiracy

When I am occasionally asked to talk about healing prayer, I typically begin by explaining that I didn't just wake up one morning and decide that learning to pray for others would be fun; I came to healing prayer through the backdoor, that is, through my own need for healing--both physical and emotional. I think it is honest to say that my conversion to Christianity at the age of 25 was due in large part to the fear that, without a loving God, I might not make it much further in life. And still, it took many years for me to realize that God is loving, that He is "for me," and not against me.

I was living in San Francisco in 1995 when I had the first ah ha experience. I had suffered for many years with respiratory ailments--chronic bronchitis, pleurisy, pneumonia, and asthma. Through a quite unexpected prophetic word from a new friend, I was told I needed to forgive my father for numerous events dating back to my childhood (Dad had died many years earlier). In a moment of frustration, I explained to God in a simple prayer that the idea of forgiving my father was not the problem--I simply didn't know how to say the words and make them stick. But pray I did--simply declaring that I forgive, and if God would do a work in my heart, it might perhaps become genuine. I went to bed that night in the early stages of a second case of pneumonia, and when I awoke in the morning, I was completely well. At the time that I spoke this prayer of forgiveness, I had no idea that it would affect my body in such a positive way. To say that my doctor was astonished is an understatement. But 'healed' I was, and though I kept thinking it would surely come back, it never has. And I did forgive my Dad, ever so slowly, slower and more labor intensive than I would have wished.

C.S. Lewis once observed that it takes courage to live through suffering, and it requires honesty to observe it. Through my experiences of healing prayer over the course of some twenty five years now, I have come to understand how our thoughts, our spiritual walk, our ability to forgive, and our willingness to give hope a second and third chance, are intricately linked to our physical health. This is what Rev. Cindy Hyde has addressed in this informative, frank and encouraging book on healing prayer. Yes, sometimes it is just a miracle; but often, healing is a journey.

In his letter to the Philippians, the Apostle Paul encourages us to meditate on that which is true, noble, what is right and pure, lovely and admirable, for these things are praiseworthy. These are also the words for healing prayer, and Jesus Christ is at the center of such things. I hope this book opens the doors to your heart, making real the love of God and that healing from heaven will be yours.

Rev. John Handley, PhD
Nacogdoches, 2015

DISCLAIMER

This book is designed to provide information on internal or emotional woundedness only. This information is provided and sold with the knowledge that the publisher and author do not offer any legal or other professional advice. In the case of a need for such expertise consult the appropriate professional. This book does not contain all information available on the subject. This book has not been created to be specific to any individual's or organizations' situation or needs. Every effort has been made to make this book as accurate as possible. However, there may be typographical and or content errors. Therefore, this book should serve only as a general guide and not as the ultimate source of subject information. This book contains information that might be dated and is intended only to educate and entertain. The author and publisher shall have no liability or responsibility to any person or entity regarding any loss or damage incurred, or alleged to have incurred, directly or indirectly, by the information contained in this book. You hereby agree to be bound by this disclaimer.

1

EXTERNAL SCARS
FROM INTERNAL WOUNDS

Tragedy has no boundaries. Traumatic events are common to mankind. Abuse abounds without respect for gender or race. Emotional or internal wounds have no boundaries or limits. We are all afflicted, troubled, abused in some way and left distressed, discouraged, and depressed.

Often one painful experience can leave us reeling in the aftereffects. The unrelenting pain of life is just too much to bear sometimes. The wounds we receive do not heal on their own, we are not taught how to process or cope with the pain that comes with life. This leaves us one option, stuff it. We can only stuff so much into our hearts and souls before we begin to think the only way we can stop the pain is to stop living.

I share many stories of those who thought there was no way out of their pain other than to stop living, and tried to end their lives, stories of those who did take their life and the impact it had on those who loved and cared about them, and stories of those who tried and did not succeed but instead found life worth living after all. These stories are meant to help you understand the effects internal wounds can have, how to get help, and how to help those who are possibly in the process of giving up. Please know above all else that there is always hope. There is always help.

"There is always help."

We all have internal wounds. Internal wounds are caused by hurtful events in our life. Internal wounds can and often do cause external scars. Let's face it, we all experience common types of internal wounds like the ones we receive from bullies as children, the awkwardness of not fitting in and being different, puberty, high school, (as if grade school was not bad enough), the boy/girlfriend that dumped us, the two-faced best friend, the co-worker that lied and got us in trouble, or worse even, that got us fired, and all the harsh words spoken to us that leave us distressed, rejected, abandoned, and neglected.

There are abuses of all kinds. Physical abuse is typically the first type of abuse we think of when we hear the word, but there are other types like spiritual abuse, mental abuse, sexual abuse, Some people experience unspeakable mistreatment, and abuse that is unthinkable. Some experiences are not only tragic but also traumatic.

We all learn to cope with the painful, hurtful or traumatic events in different ways. Some take the memories and stuff the pain down so deep into the heart that they refuse to acknowledge it, think about it, or cope with it in any way.

Others walk around with their wounds gaping and oozing. Others actually forgive what happened to them and go on with life, hurt, yes, wounded, of course, but not to the extent that the events of the past actually controls their life.

As you read this book you will find many types of internal wounds. You will see stories of those who have tried coping with their pain in unhealthy ways, and some who have found a way to cope with and bring peace to their past. My book, Making Peace with Your Past: One Choice at a Time will help you make the peace you need to make with hurtful memories and people. I also encourage you to look at each story and the chapter insights to glean from them information that will help you with your internal wounds before they turn into external scars, or before you make the decision that the only way out for you is through your death. You have options. You can get help. Always remember there are people who love you.

"You have options."

I could probably fill the whole chapter with the different types of internal wounds. You are living with them. We have all been wounded by someone haven't we? We all know people who are wounded to one degree or another. Right now I can safely say that we are all wounded. Life is just hard sometimes isn't it? Your friend or loved one may be hurting so bad right this moment that they are to the point of harming themselves and you may not even know about it.

Most deeply wounded people do not talk about their problems; they don't share their story easily, if at all. If you think your friend is suffering or hurting please try to get them to open up and talk to you. Encourage them to talk to someone else about what is going on in their life. If your friend will open up to you and share their pain or the source of their pain never judge them. You are not experiencing what they are. You do not know the level of their pain. It is real. Belittling them or judging them could be deadly. They do not need you to "fix" them by offering them all your well-meaning advice. Just listen to them. Love them through it. Be there for them.

Pain has many sources. Sometimes our pain comes through immediate family members: mother, father, sibling, aunts, uncles, grandparents, a step-parent, foster parents, adopted parents, a best friend, a lover, someone you were interested in but they were not interested in you, the one you loved that would not love you back, the one you loved who used you, a spouse, a child, a step-child, a roommate, a teacher or professor, a fellow student, a church member, a pastor, a coworker, the one who raped you, deceived you, betrayed you, got you fired… the list is almost endless. We have all heard it said, "Hurting people hurt people." It is true.

If you are hurting people, stop it! Get help. Jabez prayed a prayer, "…keep me from harm, so that I will not cause any pain." And God granted his request." (1 Chronicles 4:10 HCSB). You can pray the same prayer. You can ask the Lord to help you just like he did. You do not have to keep hurting or hurting people. Causing pain gives you control and power over the one you are hurting. Well let's just call it what it is. Abuse. You are abusing others because you were abused. Get help. You do not have to stay a victim. Nor do you have to continue to victimize others.

"Your wounds often forge your identity."

Internal wounds can leave you angry, hurt, and bitter. The wounds that go deep can often last a lifetime. The wounds can even be so deep and last so long that they become part of who you are. Your identity becomes so wrapped up in the woundedness in your soul that it becomes your normal, your reality. Your wounds often forge your identity. The wounds are part of who you are, aspects of yourself, but they do not have to define you.

Your identity should be based on something other than your opinion of yourself. Your opinion of yourself usually develops from what others have said to you or about you, or what others have done to you or not done to you. You are not who or what they say you are.

One of my clients was brutally abused as a child in just about every way imaginal. She was told she was a whore, that she was good for nothing, and that she would never be anything, never amount to anything. Such horrible words should never be spoken to another human being. These words should not be in a person's heart and should never leave a person's mouth. We need to realize there is more to what we see and hear than what we know.

She is now a grown woman, still recovering but having flashbacks and hearing the record playing in her head over and over again. "You'll never amount to anything you whore!" She has spent the majority of her life hating herself and fulfilling their prophecy over her life. She has received a great deal of healing. Her foundation is no longer based on other's opinions and words spoken over her life. Her foundational identity is now solid and firm and based on what the Word of God says about her.

"A wounded soul demands pain, even if it is your own!"

A wounded soul demands pain, even if it is your own!

Pain is demanded regardless. It seems to me that if the pain cannot be inflicted on the person who caused the wound in the first place, you will inflict pain on yourself. Self-mutilation and self-sabotaging behaviors both cause pain. One is external, the other internal. The pain is either a source of punishment or self-punishment, or a release from inner pain.

> *"We can keep the pain fresh in our minds*
> *by not forgiving the one who harmed or hurt us."*

We can keep the pain fresh in our minds by not forgiving the one who harmed or hurt us. If your wound does not heal because you refuse to forgive, then you are out for revenge and retaliation. Or at the least you want retribution, you want them to pay for what was done to you, or you want them to tell you they are sorry for what they have done. Your entire purpose in life can be to punish the person who hurt you, offended you, betrayed you, deceived you, or whatever it was they did to you whether real or imagined.

Yes, I said imagined. Sometimes our offenses are at our expense. Perhaps you misunderstood what the other person said. Was there a chance they said what they did in a tone that offended you? Maybe the other person had good intentions behind what they did or did not do? Usually not. Sometimes we can have expectations that leave us disappointed and disillusioned. We should learn how to cope with offenses so they do not leave us wounded. The most effective coping skill is to forgive. Forgive the offense. Forgive the person. Let it go.

We want to make the other person pay for what they did. When that is not possible then our pain, which is already internal or in our soul (which is the mind, will and emotions), is internalized at a deeper level. Then the demand for pain becomes so intense that you begin hurting and causing yourself pain. Or you begin hurting others. I am in no way saying that everyone who has an internal wound will physically hurt themselves but they do cause themselves emotional pain far beyond what is inflicted upon them in the first place.

Isolating ourselves is a form of self-abuse. It is also a form of self-defense from the pain and the hurt. Even the shame and guilt we saddle ourselves with is a source of continual emotional pain. Self-hatred and self-rejection are also ways we harm ourselves and inhibit the flow of love in our lives. It restricts, blocks the heart's flow just like clogged arteries of the soul block the heart's flow. We need other people in our lives.

"Our soul is our mind, will and emotions."

Emotional pain, internal wounds, soul wounds are all ways of saying the same thing. They are all wounds to the soul. Soul wounds. Our soul is our mind, will and emotions. Some souls are so wounded that they crack. They can also tear, shatter or split when people are traumatically and repetitively abused which is usually found in the ritually abused. Trauma can fragment your soul.

I worked with a young woman who had been ritualistically abused. She was shattered. She had been diagnosed with MPD (Multiple Personality Disorder) at the time. When she came to me for help she still had 16 alters. This was her reality. I did not diagnose her nor did I try to determine how many alters she had. She knew them all intimately and by name. All I knew was that she was terribly wounded and needed help. I was more than willing to allow the Lord to use me in whatever way He could to help her.

Sometimes it is not about having all the answers or all the information we need or even the training we think we need to help others. It is about us being willing to listen to others, being willing to be there for them and with them and ultimately to lead them to Christ for the answers and the direction they need.

At the time I had absolutely no experience with anyone who had MPD, which I believe is now called DID (Dissociative Identity Disorder). This fracturing of the soul is typically caused by repressed memories of sexual abuse as a child.

This does not happen to everyone because some people are just more resilient or cope with things differently. It is not a lack of coping skills that causes additional alters to be created. In fact, the creation of alters is actually a survival technique that can be quite elaborate. I have heard of cases where there were literally hundreds and even a few where there have been thousands of alters in one person before. This gives me room to believe that when abuse occurs there can be a total disassociation of you from yourself.

"We were created to love and be loved by Love Himself."

Dr. Henry Wright, in his book A More Excellent Way, shares that a breach in the relationship between you and God, you and yourself, and you and others is the cause of sickness and dis-ease in your body and mind. I found that information enlightening. In other words, we were created to be relational. We were created to love and be loved by Love Himself.

Since we are created for relationships, if there is a breach in our relationship with God, ourselves, or others we get sick. If there is a disruption or an interruption in our relationship flow, as I mentioned earlier, we get out of balance. This electro-chemical magnetically balanced disturbance or disruption in our relationships will cause our souls to become more negative. The more negative we are the sicker we can get. When we reject God and all His blessings, when we reject ourselves, and when we reject others we are really rejecting love. Without love in our lives we are pretty much doomed to a life of despair.

"Unclean spirits are real."

She and I worked together for several months with tremendous success. We examined each of the alters and worked with them individually. To our astonishment not all of the alter personalities were alters. Meaning that one of the alters was actually a demon, an unclean spirit that entered during a time when there was a great deal of sin in her life. Unclean spirits are real.

Let me explain this concept to you in a little more detail. To be able to explain them I must use the Scriptures as the ultimate Authority on them. We all know there are two realms. The physical world or realm in which we live and move and exist and then there is the supernatural realm where both good and evil exist together and influence the earthly realm. Both worlds or realms can be felt, tasted, seen, heard, and smelled.

Paranormal television shows are very popular now. Psychics are in high demand and the psychic hotlines are busy making millions. Why? We are hungry for the supernatural. We were created to relate to the supernatural.

You may be saying to yourself that you should put this book down and stop reading right now. I urge you, no; I challenge you to keep reading, at least to the end of this chapter. I share with you truth. I have lived through some amazing things and I have had more than 20 years of experience in ministry. I know the reality of what I share with you in the pages of this book. Maybe your belief system is being challenged. Maybe there is a reason you are being challenged. Don't let your doubt, your skepticism or your unbelief stop you from receiving some information that will change your life if you let it.

Unclean spirits are just that; unclean or evil spirits. They are also called demons, foul spirits, unclean spirits, impure spirits, or devils. They can walk, hear, speak, see, obey, seek, think, know and dwell in a physical body to accomplish their evil purposes (Matthew 12:43-45, Mark 1:23-24, Mark 3:11).

"Demons are evil or unclean spirits"

Bible.org states,

> Demons are evil or unclean spirits (cf. Mark 1:23 with Mark 1:32-34; Revelation 16:13-16), and are fallen angels, servants of Satan (Matthew 12:26-27; 25:41). There is only one devil, but a myriad of demons that serve the devil and make his power universal. A demoniac (Mark 5:1-20) is a person whose personality has been invaded by one or more demons, who at will can speak and act through their human victim, deranging both his mind and body.

> A number of such victims of Satan were delivered by the Servant Jesus. The unhindered power of God working through the sinless humanity of the Servant of God challenged the supernatural world of evil and explains the outburst of demonism during His earthly ministry.

The reality and personality of demons are attested in all eras of history since the Fall, as in the case of Saul and the spiritistic medium of Endor (1 Samuel 28:7-20), in the case of ancient idolatry of which demonism was the dynamic (Psalm 106:36-37; 1 Corinthians 10:20), in ancient divination and magic, and in ancient necromancy and modern spiritism.

"Prayer is the believer's resource against Satan and demons"

Demons can derange mind and body (Matthew 12:22; 17:15-18; Lk 13:16). They know the deity and lordship of Christ in the spirit world (Matthew 8:31-32; Mark 1:24; Acts 19:15; Jas 2:19), and realize their predestined fate (Matthew 8:31-32; Lk 8:31). They have a conspicuous role in the government of the Satanic world system (Daniel 10:13; Ephesians 6:12), in promoting cultism and false doctrine (1 Timothy 4:1-3), and in opposing God's program and God's people (Ephesians 6:12; 1 John 4:1-6). Prayer is the believer's resource against Satan and demons (Ephesians 6:10-20). (Unknown. Retrieved on July, 18, 2015 from
https://bible.org/illustration/unclean-spirits).

There is no fear where demons are concerned. You should never fear them. You should fear only what God can do to you. Fear, reverence, and respect for God.

As a minister, I learned many lessons from my time with the young woman diagnosed with DID. Together we prayed our way through her pain. We worked through layers of abuse, some horrific memories, all the while asking for the guidance of the Holy Spirit and the intervention of the Lord Jesus. He was faithful to guide us and help us every step of the way.

11

One of the main things, I believe, that made the difference in her healing was connecting her to the presence of Jesus Christ as she revisited each memory. We learned that each memory has a belief system attached to it. Each of the belief systems led to a feeling or thoughts. Those thoughts or feelings directed her actions. As each memory was visited, each belief system corrected with the truth, and each one connected to Jesus, the healing manifested. Meaning she was totally integrated.

"Jesus came to heal the brokenhearted."

I am very proud to say that this young woman left her alternative lifestyle and unhealthy relationship. She is now a credentialed and ordained minister in a large denominational church serving the Lord and giving back to society by helping others. There are just some things therapy cannot help with. There is pain that only Jesus can heal. Jesus came to heal the brokenhearted. (Luke 4:18)

"There is always hope in Jesus."

There is a faith-based Christ-centered therapy called Theophostic Prayer developed by Dr. Ed Smith. He learned to connect people to the presence of Jesus for their ultimate healing. (The contact information is in the Resource section at the back of this book.) He said he could tell them the truth, they could receive the truth, recognize the truth, but still not make the connection that brought change. He worked with incest survivors. It was not until he began connecting them to the Presence of Jesus that their lives began to change as He healed their hearts. There is always hope in Jesus. It does not matter what you have been through.

"Our behavior is often driven by our pain."

Our behavior is often driven by our pain. We feel what we believe. We act out what we feel. When we are wounded and those wounds never heal, they are open and oozing and susceptible to infection and be reinjured. How many times have you had a sore finger or thumb and hit is every time you turn around? Or how many times have you stumped your toe only to keep injuring it while it is still injured adding pain on top of the pain already there.

As a Paramedic I understood the principles of physical injuries and the dynamics of pain. We were equipped to provide protection for the injury as to prevent infection and further injury either by cleaning and bandaging the wound, applying pressure to control bleeding, or by stabilizing a broken bone. In our souls these same types of wounds happen.

"...first aid also needs to be applied to the soul."

First aid for the body is one thing but first aid also needs to be applied to the soul. For healing to begin there needs to be an application of 'first aid' in the form of someone validating our feelings or our wound, in the form of someone listening to us and saying they are sorry.

The old saying, "Sticks and stones may break my bones, but words will never hurt me" is a lie. Words can hurt deeper and much longer than a broken bone. Broken bones heal in six weeks. But how long has your heart been broken? A broken heart can last a life-time, but it does not have to stay broken. There is healing for a broken heart, a broken spirit, a shattered soul, or a wounded spirit.

There are wounds that are common to man. We have all been given a way to find healing for our wounds. In the pages of this book you will find many methods you can use to find help and healing. You do not have to stay wounded. I am not saying that the memories can be taken away; I am saying the memories can be healed. The pain of the abuse can be healed. As Caroline Myss (2011) so eloquently wrote,

> We are not meant to stay wounded. We are supposed to move through our tragedies and challenges and to help each other move through the many painful episodes of our lives. By remaining stuck in the power of our wounds, we block our transformation. We overlook the greater gifts inherent in our wounds — the strength to overcome them and the lessons that we are meant to receive through them. Wounds are the means through which we enter the hearts of other people. They are meant to teach us to become compassionate and wise.

2

MY SON CUT HIS THROAT

I received a phone call no parent would ever expect. And one no parent could ever prepare for.

"Shawn slit his throat!" The voice on the other end of the phone said. I could not believe I just heard those words. I am always getting things jumbled up in my head. I thought I had really heard that one wrong for sure.

"What? I don't think I heard you right."

Again, "Cindy, Shawn slit his throat." Again I heard the words I did not want to hear. I was in shock. I still could not believe what I heard was really what I heard. They proceeded to tell me where they were taking my son, but I could not hear clearly with my mind fixed on the words that had pierced my heart so deeply.

Was he dead? Was he alive? A terror struck my heart in

that instant that can never be undone.

Hearing those words echo in my mind like a nonstop record over and over again brought a heartache with them that was so deep it is indescribable.

What do you do when you hear those words? Or words similar to them? Words that your loved one is injured, hurt, dead?

Cry. Absolutely!

Ask God WHY? Absolutely!

Being a Paramedic we learn about the Golden Hour. When someone is traumatized there is a 60 minute window for emergency medical help to arrive, provide medical help and transport the traumatized person to the hospital. Chances of survival are dramatically decreased after the Golden Hour. The first hour is always the most important time in a crisis.

My son was out in the woods checking on a potential job. He was with his dad and another man. He was sitting in the truck. His dad had just stepped out of the truck to talk to the other man. They had only visited for a few minutes when the man said, "Hey, Shawn just cut his throat!"

His dad ran to him, took a shirt and attempted to wrap it around Shawn's neck. Shawn wrestled with his dad. He did not want him helping him.

The other man called 911. They were out so far that the man had to drive 80 and 90 miles an hour for 10 miles to even get where there was an address so he could meet the ambulance and guide them to where Shawn was.

When the ambulance arrived they stabilized my son as much as possible. We are already close to the 30 minute mark. They called the helicopter for him to be life-flighted. They made it to the hospital with him before the Golden Hour was up.

"Was he alive or was he dead?"

It was during this first 60 minutes of hearing that my son had slit his throat that my heart was unbearably breaking. Still I questioned, 'Was he alive or was he dead?' I could not find the answer. I could not find my son.

I could not understand what hospital they said he was being life-flighted to. I could not find the number to the hospitals in the town they said he was going to because I could not see. The tears were streaming down my face like an overflowing dam. I could not comprehend what people around me were saying.

I was experiencing a nervous breakdown for the first time in my life. I could barely breathe. My breaths were shallow and irregular, mostly holding my breath in unbelief. I tried to walk and almost collapsed. My teeth were literally and visibly chattering like I was freezing. I was in shock. I am a strong woman, I can handle pressure, and I can handle crisis situations. I am usually the one who calms others down. I was not so strong when I heard this news.

I could barely see but I managed to send out a few text messages through the hot searing tears. I also put a prayer request out on Facebook. Some people are private about their lives. I happen to believe in support, in getting help when you need it. I am an open book. If the things I go through can somehow help others see and learn from the way the Lord in dealing with the situation then I am happy to help. At that point in time I was determined to get as many people as I could possibly mobilized praying for my son. I know there were upwards of 50,000 people praying for him and for our family at one time. That is some powerful spiritual support. We all need some type of support group when we experience a crisis don't we?

"Prayer support is vital during a crisis."

When the phone rang at one point I just handed the phone to my husband because I just could not stop crying long enough to talk. I could barely breathe let alone talk. My friend heard me weeping and just began to pray. He prayed in the Spirit and commanded an anointing of peace to come over me. It did. Within minutes the sobbing had subsided for the most part, my heart stopped racing away, I began to breathe easier, and I could actually start thinking and processing what people were saying again. Prayer support is vital during a crisis.

"You are never really alone."

My friend's prayers, combined with all the other prayer support pulled my son, me, and my family through one of the darkest hours of our lives. I cannot emphasize how important it is to have a strong support group. You do not have to belong to a church to have a support group. I know social media was one of the avenues I used to connect because I know how effective it is. It does not matter what is going on in your life, there is always someone to help you if you reach out for it. There is always someone who will understand what you are going through. You are never really alone.

One of our other sons (we have three) called and found Shawn for us. He was at the hospital (a different one than I was initially told). He was still in surgery. My reckoning was that if he was still in surgery he was still alive. At least for now, my son was still alive. He was alive!

We got the information we needed for the trip and immediately left to be by his side. We experienced many challenges on the way as you can imagine. Getting turned around, storms, and wrecks… nothing was going to keep us from our son.

When we arrived we saw him lying in the bed. His face was pale. He eyes were distant. IVs were running to replace some of the blood he lost. The three lengthy slits on his throat spoke volumes. 27 external metal stitches. He cut 13 inches across his throat from one ear to the other. We do not know how many internal stitches they put in. I did not ask him why he did what he did. I was just there with him and for him. I figured there would be time for all the questions in my heart to be answered later.

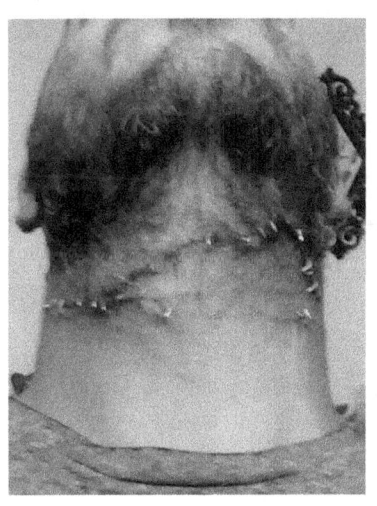

As we were visiting him we found out that after he cut his throat he leaned his head back and took a picture with his cell phone. A picture of his slit throat? What in the world? A reminder of the internal conflict inside his soul?

The external scars this event will leave are going to be very visible and very obvious to everyone who sees him. He is going to have to answer the question, 'What happened to you?' for the rest of his life. He is going to see it in the mirror

19

every day of his life. A constant reminder of one of life's defining moments that changed the direction of his life forever.

I know of others who have taken pictures of their self-mutilation, he is not alone in this. I did not understand why he would do such a thing until I started doing some research on the subject of self-mutilation and self-harming. In some cases it is a reminder of what they did. You will read the story of a very young woman who will remain anonymous for obvious reasons in the next few chapters that will bring more clarity to this subject matter of cutting and taking pictures of it.

Through the audible experience of hearing the report and the visual experience of seeing my son lying there in the hospital with his wounds made me all the more aware of the internal wounds that cause our external scars.

"I am forever scarred emotionally by those words and the images of my son's throat, but I am healed and walk in peace now."

"Shawn slit his throat!" Echoes in my mind. This became one of my internal wounds. I am forever scarred by those words and the images of my son's throat. However, there is peace after tragedy. Let me explain how I found peace. First of all I had a very strong support group who covered me in prayer.

Secondly, I had a very strong faith in Jesus Christ as my Lord and Savior and an unwavering belief that God's promises are for me. He promised me that because I love Him He would work everything out for my good. He promised me that He would perfect that which concerns me. When you have confidence, belief, and faith in a God who makes those kinds of promises the only thing you need to do when a crisis comes into your life is keep focused. That's right. Focus on God. I do not say that flippantly. It was hard for me to get focused when the news came. There was about an hour that I was upset beyond belief as my soul reeled from the impact, then it was simply a matter of remembering Whose I was and the promises that I have been given. The shift in my mindset or in my thinking was the key to me walking in victory and in peace.

I have a choice. So do you. I can choose to be thankful and grateful that my son's life was spared. We are all grateful that he missed every vital organ and will not suffer any permanent physical damage. I can also choose to allow those words "Shawn slit his throat" to pass by as I hear them in my mind instead of entertaining them. This is how you can gain and maintain peace through it all.

We have the ability to control what we think about. I choose to think about the abundant life he is going to live now that he is getting some help. I choose to think in the future not in the past. I choose to receive the miracle and give thanks. So can you. There is help and there is always hope. Don't give in to the thoughts of helplessness and hopeless, thought of despair and darkness. Let the Light begin to shine in your dark time of life.

It was the internal wounds in my son's soul that caused him to self-mutilate and attempt to take his life. The internal wounds were so gaping and he was so emotionally raw that he took a dull knife to his throat and began to cut himself from one ear to the other.

"...it was a miracle."

The miracle of this event is not only that he survived it, but that he survived with no permanent damage. Except for the shocking external scar he will always have to look at as a reminder of his pain. He did not cut any major organs, nerves, veins or arteries. Had he actually cut his jugular, there would have been no saving his life. He would have bled out before the ambulance got to him. The doctor said he missed it by 1/8 of an inch. The surgeon agreed it was a miracle.

Chapter Insights

So why did he do this?

He says he does not know why. He said he was sitting in the truck, looked down, saw the knife, and started cutting.

I asked him what he was thinking right before he did that. He said, "Mom, I wasn't thinking about anything. I just saw the knife, picked it up, and started cutting."

After a day or so I sent him a text message asking him if death was his intention or was it just a deep seated self-loathing.

He replied, "Just wanted to stop being here, doing this going nowhere, hopelessness I think. Ummm, I took the easy way out mom. Turns out that was the hard way but, I'm not the feelers type of guy to be able to explain why I did what I did. Mostly on impulse."

I believe him. I believe it was on an impulse. However, I know there were things going on in his life the past three years that greatly influenced his 'impulsive' decision. I have learned that most of the suicides that occur are impulsive or spontaneous.

"You should not stuff them away and never talk about them."

He was wounded by several major life-altering events that he had little control over. They were heavy emotional things people just do not get over easily. Things he blames himself for. Things he feels guilty for. We all have those kinds of things in our lives don't we? What do we do with them? I can tell you what you should not do. You should not stuff them away and never talk about them. Believe it or not, talking helps get the problem out of you.

Talking about what is going on in your life can actually help you realize some other things about the way you feel or about the events that have happened. Perhaps you can even begin seeing them through different lenses. Sometimes others can help you by pointing out things you never would have thought about before. Especially if the someone you talk to is a professional. But you do not always need to seek professional help, sometimes it is expensive or you think you do not need the help, but you do need to talk to someone. This is why stuffing or internalizing your pain, your woundedness and suffering alone is never a good idea.

Open up. Don't be afraid.

"Emotional pain is a common denominator..."

Internal wounds. We all have them. Emotional pain is a common denominator for the human race. We all experience it to one degree or another. What makes the difference is how we deal or cope with the pain. Some stuff it. Some let it out in healthy ways, like seeking counsel, therapy, support groups, or other kinds of help. Some let it out in unhealthy ways like cutting, drinking, drugs, sex, and other means of self-abuse to escape or momentarily dull the pain. The pain never leaves in this type of coping. The problems are only compounded by new problems caused by the unhealthy behaviors.

Sometimes the internal wounds leave external scars for others to see. Cut wrists, cut throats, as in my son's case, gunshot suicides that go awry and leave the face horribly scarred, are all external scars that show the degree of internal pain inside the soul.

Drugs, substance abuse of all kinds and alcohol also leave external scars. Sometimes not in the same way as suicide attempts or cutting. For example, someone gets drunk and falls down injuring themselves. They find relationships that will only validate the hate they already have for themselves. They lie, cheat, steal, deceive, and often bring ruin not only to themselves but to their families. They often live life for the next fix, the next drink, or the next relationship.

"Some are too afraid to report the abuse"

How many others are harmed because people choose to take mind-altering substances? Some of the ones that are injured by those taking something make it to the hospital. Some never do. Some are too afraid to report the abuse. Others silently live with the abuser hoping against all hope that it will get better and that they will change. The statistics are staggering I am sure.

My parents were enablers. I watched them live their lives in fear and often in lack as they paid bail bondsmen and suffered because their money was stolen. Not just in fear for the possessions, which they lost a great deal of both cash and jewelry, but fear for their lives. Fear of being burned to death because of the cigarettes that fell in the bed and on the floor. Fear because they never knew when their child was going to be sober or under the influence. In fact, they had two children who inflicted fear in their hearts because of internal woundedness.

The fact is many elderly people either live with their abusive children, or the abusive children live with them. Either way their abuse rarely gets reported.

Here are nine types of abuse:

1. Physical Abuse
2. Sexual Abuse, Rape, or Molestation
3. Emotional, Mental, or Psychological Abuse
4. Neglect, Self-Neglect, or Abandonment
5. Financial or Material Exploitation
6. Spiritual or Religious Abuse
7. Verbal Abuse
8. Hate Crimes
9. Cultural Violence
10. Cult Abuse

If you know of someone who is being abused it is your moral duty to report it. Do the right thing. Contact the National Center on Elder Abuse, Administration on Aging at 1-800-677-1116 or http://www.ncea.aoa.gov.

Those who have deep internal wounds often cause themselves external scars by the things they do to themselves. Sometimes the external scars are not on them; often those external scars are on the ones that love those who are wounded. They cause external scars from the wounds that are inflicted upon others by them. For example, a parent, a child, a girlfriend or boyfriend, spouse and even a friend can wound us.

My sibling was so combative under the influence of alcohol that there are several Police Officers with external scars now because of her internal wounds.

Many sons and daughters have been orphaned and many spouses have been left widowed because of their reckless behavior or because of someone else's reckless, irresponsible, and thoughtless behavior.

I understand that sometimes the internal pain in your soul can hurt so intensely that all you can think about is the pain. You cannot and often do not think of others. Unless it is the one(s) who hurt you. You cannot and often do not even think of yourself. Your focus is on getting relief from the pain. Even if that relief comes in the form of taking your life. Let me tell you this, taking your life effects everyone around you. You may not be able to see it right now but it does.

One of the comments my son made while he was in the hospital, surrounded by family, "I did not know how loved I was." Did you see what he said? He had no idea he was loved. He also did not realize how many people needed him. His family rallied around him in his time of personal crisis. He said he felt very selfish afterwards. He said he felt so bad for costing everyone money and causing everyone to drive for hours just to see about him. That is what love does though. It goes the extra mile.

What if he had asked for help or reached out to someone for help when he realized how depressed or hopeless he felt. For many, reaching out is not something that happens until after the fact. Please reach out to someone if you are depressed or hurting. Getting help is not embarrassing. It does not make you weak, in fact, only intelligent people can figure out that they need help and get it.

Be smart! Get help.

You deserve it.

There are people in this world that love you.

3

FATAL ACCIDENT WITH A DRUNK DRIVER TAKES TWO LIVES

Returning from a singing late one evening, Michael, his wife, step-daughter and another friend were in a fatal head-on collision with a drunk driver. Two cars were coming over the hill at the same time; the cops said they were playing chicken. The vehicle in the oncoming lane had their headlights on but the one coming straight at him did not have headlights on. Michael, who is now my husband, was driving the van. He did everything he could to avoid the collision, but even his best was not good enough in this case. There was no escaping the collision with the oncoming car. The fatal crash was simply unavoidable.

The crash instantly killed the young man driving the car that hit them. The impact was so hard it broke the bolts in the passenger's seat where Michael's wife sat. She was ejected out of the vehicle and through the windshield. They said she died instantly.

Her 18 year old daughter was with them, sitting in the back seat. They said her neck was snapped and that it killed her instantaneously. The officials said that neither of the women suffered and perhaps never even felt pain.

"Their future was violently ripped from them"

Both of these women were beautiful, loving and talented. They were full of life and enriched the lives of all those who knew them. Both of them had a bright and promising future ahead of them. Their future was violently ripped from them.

There was also another passenger who was also severely injured and she survived. She also had to be air-flighted. She had to have several surgeries. The event left her with many external wounds as a constant reminder of the young man who was emotionally or internally wounded enough to escape his problems by drinking then getting behind the wheel of the vehicle.

Michael had to be life-flighted to a regional trauma center where he spent eleven days in ICU recovering before being released to a regular room for many more days. He had a broken collar bone, three broken ribs, a collapsed lung, head trauma, a shattered ankle that they had to be repaired with screws, and cuts all over his body from the shattered glass from the windshield. His internal wounds were more serious than his external wounds, even though they were life-threatening.

Chapter Insights

The external scars are all over my husband's body serve as a constant reminder of that tragic night. His internal or emotional wounds from such a devastating and tragic accident were much more serious than the life-threatening ones he recovered from physically. His pain is not always present, he is not always thinking about the wreck or his loss, but there are so many times he has flashbacks caused by seeing a similar vehicle to the one he was driving that night. And he has nightmares as he relives the traumatic event in the night hours. And from people driving without their headlights on. It never fails when we are out after dark that we always see someone driving without their lights on. Because of this drunk driver he is scarred for life inside and out.

"I think Jesus Christ is the Healer"

They say time heals. I think time can dull the pain. It can give us the space we need to mature and heal from the pain. I do not think time itself is a healer. I believe Jesus Christ is our Healer. "..God anointed Jesus of Nazareth with the Holy Spirit and power, and how he went around doing good and healing all who were under the power of the devil, because God was with him." (Acts 10:38 NIV) There is more than ample evidence of this fact. Miracles are real. I have experienced them in my own life and I have seen many of them. Miraculous healings like the blind see, the deaf hear, the lame walk, and the broken-hearted are healed.

The only way to ever be completely healed is to believe in and trust Jesus to heal your broken heart and heal your wounds. He has healed mine. He has healed Michael's and the boys, and he has healed hundreds that I have worked with over the years. He wants to heal your broken heart (your emotional or soul wounds).

The crash not only affected those who were in it, but it also affected two small sons who would have been killed in the crash had they been with them that night. The boys were six years old and eight years old at the time of the accident. It affected her other son and all the other family members and the many friends they had. It even affected the church she pastored and the singing group she had. Whenever we make a decision, we must always count the cost. Everything we do has an effect on those around us.

This is only one story out of thousands every year that are caused by people who have internal wounds and choose to self-destruct through drugs or alcohol.

The young man was responsible for taking the lives of two beautiful and talented women that night and leaving two tender young boys without a mother and without a sister.

"Our actions always affect others."

It was the young man driving the car that night, over a hill without headlights who was wounded internally to the point that he risked not only his life and the life of his friend, but also the life of anyone on the road that night. He may not have set out on the mission of killing himself or anyone else that night, but he chose to drive while under the influence. His behavior spoke loudly. Actions always speak louder than words don't they? Our actions always affect others.

Driving while influenced by alcohol or other drugs is risky behavior. Accidents are caused by drivers under the influence on an hourly basis. According to the United States Department of Transportation three people are killed in alcohol-related highway accidents every 2 hours. (Chambers, Liu, & Moore, 2012). How many lives is that in one 24 hour day? 36 people per day. And that is just counting alcohol-related crashes.

"On average, a pedestrian was killed every two hours and injured every nine minutes in traffic crashes" (USDTS, Pedestrians, 2009). Not to be gruesome but that is 4 lives taken every two hours and countless injuries from accidents. These statistics are just the ones that involve vehicles.

Please hear this plea from the wife of a man with two small children whose life was heartbreakingly changed forever because of a drunk driver, please never drink or do drugs of any kind and get behind the wheel of a vehicle. Never drive unless you are sober.

There is always someone willing to take you home. Find a way.

"Do not risk the lives of others."

Don't risk your life. Do not risk the lives of others. Do not drink and drive. You do not understand the devastation of two young boys having to live with the loss of their mother like I do. You do not understand the heart cry of a man whose wife was tragically jerked from this world. If you don't care about yourself, at least care about the ones you might hurt if you drive under the influence.

You do not know the fear of the one who was driving and survived a wreck when they have to get behind the wheel of a vehicle and drive again. You don't know and cannot possibly understand the night terrors, the flash-backs and the panic they both bring with them as they re-experience the crash time and time again.

First of all I beg you to reach out to someone and get some help for your internal woundedness. It is not just an addiction that you face; it is trying to drown out the pain of something tragic that happened to you. It is the pain of being abused in some way or in every sort of way that causes you to want to be numb, to escape your reality. It is the pain of losing a loved one that causes you to self-medicate. It is the unforgiveness, the shame, the guilt, the self-condemnation you feel towards yourself that causes you to stay wounded. These are all different types of internal wounds and there are many more but the main point is that no matter how deeply you are wounded you are not alone and you are loved. Help is available.

I am sure you know by now the fact that there is no food, drink, drug, activity, or person that can make you love yourself or make you like what you see in the mirror in the morning. Only through the affirmation of yourself through God, family, and friends can you change how you see or feel about yourself.

If you are interested in receiving help here is a list of places to reach out to.

- 24 Hour Addiction Helpline: 888-327-5040

- Alcohol Anonymous: http://www.aa.org/

- Celebrate Recovery: http://www.celebraterec overy.com/cr-groups/group-locator

4

MY FRIEND PULLED THE TRIGGER

My cherished friend had internal wounds that never healed. The problem they had was partly caused by the internal lies they believed. They were frequently depressed but oh how they loved their children and their family.

They went to their parent's house one day to visit their children. Everything seemed to be ok. They seemed like things were going good, but they weren't doing good.

Early one morning they took a gun, put it to their head and pulled the trigger. The parents and his children were in the next room. My friend's life ended. The lives of those children and the parents who loved their child so deeply were tragically changed in that instant. There were no warning signs. No goodbyes.

How does a mother, a father, a child cope with the loss of their loved one when something like this happens?

Just the mess that was left behind was horrifying. Who cleaned all that up? Did the parents have to clean it up? Either way these parents have to live in the house with a constant reminder that their child took their life right there in their home.

I know the impact of that one gunshot echoes in their souls over and over again. I also know that their hearts are pierced time and again when they even hear a gun go off. Sounds, smells, sights are powerful triggers. Ones that can cause an untold amount of grief alone.

Chapter Insights

Grief stricken, sad beyond comprehension and forever left internally wounded, these parents, the children, and all the other loved ones had to pick up the pieces and continue living their lives.

I know they had questions like, "Why didn't we know what was going to happen?"

"Wasn't there something I could have said or done that would have made a difference?"

Statements like, "This is my fault! If I had been a better mother/father this would not have happened."

I am telling you these are common questions that are typically asked when something like this happens. However, the answers are usually never found. Unless the person is open and exhibiting signs that something is really wrong there is not much of anything anyone can do. Unless, of course, they reach out for help you. One of the purposes of this book is to encourage those who are hurting to reach out and not suffer silently like my friend did. Like my son did. Like my brother did. Like my daughter-in-law did.

I believe in this case there were unhealed interior wounds. But what if there was a darker force was at work. What if what they experienced was a moment of emotional weakness that opened a door?

"...there were demonic forces..."

My experience in the supernatural realm confirms to me that there were demonic forces that caused my friend to do what they did. I am not saying that my friend was demon possessed. Since most suicides are spontaneous I do not believe there was a plan for taking their life. They thought about it long enough to know to get the gun and I know they had to think about where they would act on their thoughts. I am saying there was demonic influence.

Demonic influence is often unnoticed. Mistaken for internal thoughts. Voices that sound like you, sound like they come from you, but they do not originated from within you. They are suggested thoughts. Depressing thoughts, self-hatred thoughts, thoughts of harming yourself or others, thoughts of hopelessness and helplessness are common thoughts whispered into the mind by unclean spirits. I am not saying every thought you have comes from unclean spirits, but these kinds of thoughts originate from unclean sources. I am saying they put the thoughts into our minds and we are the ones who choose to entertain them and accept them as truths or not.

"I believe these choices were also demonically influenced."

Why did my friend make the choice to take their life inside the house with his parents and children home? Why didn't he do what they thought must done in the woods or somewhere else? I believe these choices were also demonically influenced.

Perhaps they hated his parents and wanted to punish them for some wrong or perceived wrong. I can buy that, I get it. But to do that to their children? I cannot believe they would do that to them if they had a sound mind and had the ability to think rationally. If they had emotional stability they would not have taken their life in the first place.

"They become narcissistic."

I have come to understand that by the time a person has gone from despair and depression to thinking and planning about their death they are not thinking about others. They are thinking of themselves. Their thinking is consumed by their pain so much so that it causes them to be self-absorbed. They are no longer thinking about how their loved ones might feel or what they might have to go through if they took their own life. They become narcissistic.

"A narcissist is not a bad person."

Do not be offended at the word narcissist here. A narcissist is someone who withdraws and isolates because of their internal woundedness.

> According to Dr. Samuel López De Victoria, Ph.D., (2014), "Extreme narcissists tend to be persons who move towards eventually cutting others off and becoming emotionally isolated. Their internal wounds have caused them to look inside themselves for so long there is not much room in their heart or in the mind for much else."

Narcissists were wounded as children. As adults they are usually still bleeding. Dr. López De Victoria, (2014) states the "trauma was devastating to the point it almost killed that person emotionally. They are protecting themselves." Moreover, a narcissist will create false personas for protection (think of a turtle shell where they can come in and out but no one else can get in). They thwart any potential chance of a relationship developing which might lead to more pain. A narcissist is not a bad person. They just live "in an emotional and relational fort of isolation" (López De Victoria, 2014).

"We are all wounded. We are all hurt."

Let's get real. We are all wounded. We are all hurt. We are all in pain emotionally from something that happened to us. We are all afraid of something, especially of getting hurt again. We all have fears that we must live with.

Merle Shain (1985) explains that we only really have two fears: The fear from the original wound and the fear of "giving up our defenses and having to face the wild arrows of pain" (p. 33. para. 2).

In other words, fear penetrates our hearts or comes into our soul when the original wound is inflicted. The other fear comes from the thought of the event happening again. Shain explains that our fear is like a roadblock in life (1985). One that we care for and use to protect ourselves with lest we let our wall of defense down and let the pain crash into our soul again.

"The original or the first wound never completely goes away."

The original or the first wound never completely goes away. The pain can never be buried deep enough that there is no trace of it. Our pain forges us into fearful individuals who hide our authentic selves safely away from the pain, but in reality, the pain paralyzes us, keeps us from truly living.

In her book, Hearts That We Broke Long Ago, Merle Shain (1985) wrote,

> We all carry the cross-hatching of a thousand wounds. The wounds of childhood, still bleeding like the signs of the stigmata. The wounds of adolescence, still stinging with remembered pain. The bitter wounds of adult failures, or soured loved and lost dreams.
>
> How to make them all go away? How to become brave and young again? How to wipe the slate clean and reenter the world like a tabula rasa, trusting and trustworthy again? I wish I knew.
>
> I only know the answer doesn't lie in learning how to protect yourself from life. It lies in learning how to strengthen yourself so you can let a bit more of it in (p. 34, para. 2).

"…the fear of what may happen is infinitely worse"

We try to protect ourselves but to what extent are we successful? Somewhat, a little, not at all? And what price do we as individuals pay for the protection we convince ourselves we need and from what is it that we think we are protecting ourselves from? It is my experience that the fear of what may happen is infinitely worse that what actually happens.

"Sometimes the one we need protection from is our self."

Sometimes the one we need protection from is our self. Seriously. Think about it. Have you not heard, "We are our own worst enemy." How many times have you hurt yourself? Perhaps not physically but think about how many times your internal wounds and the fears they brought with them have caused you to sabotage jobs, relationships, advancements, finances, friendships, and most of all love? We do this to ourselves. And why? I think partly because we do not think we deserve any better.

Somewhere and at some time we are told a lie. We internalize that lie, whatever it is, and that one lie begins to shape our identity. A young woman hears the words from a bully at school, "You're so ugly." Or perhaps they hear these words, "You're fat." Even if the girl was ugly or even if she was fat, being told something from someone who means us harm does harm us internally.

"Words hurt…"

That old saying, "Sticks and stones may break my bones, but words will never hurt me" is a harsh lie. Words hurt much worse and for much longer than broken bones. Verbal abuse affects every area of our life. They cause wounds that may not be externally visible, but their damage is devastating.

Internal wounds from words, from verbal abuse, can stay open and bleeding throughout our lives. Causing us to continually favor that spot in fear of further wounding. Always believing whatever lie was told us. Where is the truth? For me, it was found in the Scriptures. The truth about me and the truth for me.

"Seven truths you can start believing right now"

Here are seven truths about you that can you start believing right now.

Truth #1: You have value and worth beyond measure.

Truth #2: You are an original and unique masterpiece.

Truth #3: You are important and significant.

Truth #4: You possess the power to create or destroy your world.

Truth # 5: You can take control of your thoughts and steer yourself in the right direction.

Truth #6: You are designed for success and engineered for greatness.

Truth #7: You have a special skill set, talents and abilities. Your potential is unlimited.

Believing a lie, any lie, will keep you in prison. Richard Lovelace in his poem wrote, "Stone walls does not a prison make, nor iron bars a cage." When I first heard this it impacted my life so strongly that after more than 15 years I have used it in three of my books. The reality: We make our own prisons! We imprison ourselves, not with stone walls or iron bars but with lies. We imprison ourselves with our thoughts. With our faulty belief systems.

Not only have we imprisoned ourselves, while we sit in our prison of lies, negative thoughts, and faulty belief systems, we torture ourselves. That's right. We torture ourselves. Don't tell me you have never done this before. Inside. Not outwardly most of the time, but it is when this happens that the external scars are formed. We torture ourselves when we bully ourselves. We torture ourselves when we repeat over and over in our minds a traumatic event that happened to us. Or when someone was abusive to us and we just can't let it go. We also abuse ourselves when we do something wrong and do not forgive ourselves for it. We have all done this. We all do this. It is not healthy.

There are some skills that will help stop the vicious cycle of self-abuse. You can learn to remove the stones you have put around your heart and set yourself free by changing the way you think. You can replace the lies you believe with truths about yourself and that will also set you free. You can forgive yourself.

"We all need to forgive ourselves."

We have all done things we need to forgive ourselves for. It was the hardest thing I have ever done in my life. Forgive myself. It is possible to forgive yourself. I did, and it changed my life. You need to know the reality about forgiveness. There is only one sin that is unforgivable and that is the sin is the blasphemy of the Holy Spirit (Matthew 12:31). It was not until the sin of unforgiveness was dealt with in my own life that I could begin the healing journey.

We are often our own worst enemy. Shawn is a perfect example of a wounded soul that needed to receive forgiveness and to extend forgiveness to himself. Those internal wounds have now caused some extensive external scars that he will have to see every day of his life. Scars that people will ask about. Scars that will be a constant reminder of one of the darkest hours of his life. Simply because he has internal wounds that have not yet healed. I know he will have to come to a place where he will have to forgive himself for what he has done to himself, and to others.

He did renounce death and choose life. It is important to understand that once the enemy has a foothold in your life in this area of self-harm, self-mutilation, cutting, suicide it is a strong one.

"He chose death over life."

Many times we need deliverance from the demons they are fighting with. Sometimes we can simply undo what has been done by choosing the opposite of what they chose in the first place. Like Shawn did. He chose death over life. He repented and then he chose to live life instead of dying.

Forever those choices are in front of us. Many times I have been confronted with the choice of life or death. I chose. The thought of death for me is not frightening, but death is permanent.

"Our authentic self is the person we were created to be."

Often feelings of self-hatred and self-loathing happen when our authentic self clashes with our fantasy self. We all have those conflicts of identity. 'Who am I?' is a common question. Other common questions are 'why am I here?' 'What is my purpose?' Our authentic self is the person we were created to be.

Even at our worst we are still wonderfully and marvelously created and knit together and formed in our mother's womb and made in the image of God. God saw what He created and said it was good.

It is the enemy of our soul who wants to twist and contort our image into something other than what God created it to be. We have all heard the saying about God not creating junk. It is true. We often base who we think we are on who everyone around us thinks we are. That is not always a good or positive thing to do. Your identity however is never and will never be based on what you think of yourself or what others think of you. It is based simply on the facts, on the truth.

To read about your creation story find a Bible and read in Genesis. You might just be amazed to find out how fearfully and wonderfully made you actually are. Let me just say that there is a reality beyond what we can see. There is a spiritual reality as well.

If you are an agnostic or an atheist then skip over that part. It still does not negate the reality of who you are. Or that your identity is not what this world, your family, or you say it is.

Read these ancient words of wisdom from a King named David in the next chapter. They will encourage you and give you some things to seriously consider concerning your reality.

5

YOU KNOW ALL ABOUT ME
David

You may not realize it yet, but there is someone in your life who knows all about you. That someone is the same Someone Who created you. Read what King David said in this ancient text translated into modern language.

For the Pure and Shinning One,
King David's poetic song.

[1]Lord, You know everything there is to know about me.
You've examined my innermost being
with Your loving gaze.
[2]You perceive every movement of my heart and soul,
And understand my every thought
Before it even enters my mind!
[3-4] You are so intimately aware of me, Lord,
You read my heart like an open book

And You know all the words I'm about to speak
Before I even start a sentence!
You know every step I will take,
Before my journey even begins!

⁵You've gone into my future to prepare the way,
And in kindness You follow behind me
To spare me from the harm of my past.
With Your hand of love upon my life,
You imparted a Father's blessing to me!
⁶This is just too wonderful,
Deep and incomprehensible!
Your understanding of me brings wonder and strength.

⁷Where could I go from Your Spirit?
Where could I run and hide from Your face?
⁸If I got up to heaven, You're there!
If I go down to the realm of the dead, You're there too!
⁹If I fly with wings into the shining dawn, You're there!
If I fly into the radiant sunset, You're there waiting!
¹⁰Wherever I go Your hand will guide me,
Your strength will empower me.
¹¹It's impossible to disappear from You
Or to ask the darkness to hide me,
For Your presence is everywhere
Bringing light into my night!

¹²There is no such thing as darkness with You.
The night, to You, is as bright as the day;
There's no difference between the two!

¹³You formed my innermost being,
Shaping my delicate inside, And my intricate outside,
And wove them all together in my mother's womb.
¹⁴I thank You God, for making me so mysteriously
complex!
Everything you do is marvelously breathtaking!

It simply amazes me to think about it!
How thoroughly you know me, Lord!
[15]You even shaped every bone in my body,
When You created me in the secret place,
Carefully, skillfully shaping me
From nothing to something!
[16]You saw who You created me to be,
Before I became me!
Before I'd ever seen the light of day,
The number of days You planned for me,
Were all recorded in Your book.

[17-18]Every single moment You are thinking of me!
How precious and wonderful to consider,
That You cherish me constantly in Your every thought!
O God, Your desires [thoughts] toward me are more
Than the grains of sand on every shore!
When I awake each morning, You're still thinking of me.

[23]God, I invite Your searching gaze into my heart.
Examine me through and through,
Find out everything
That may be hidden within me.
Psalm 139

When you read the words King David wrote thousands of years ago you should feel the reality of his song stirring in your heart. He sings about how God knows your thoughts. You are an open book to Him. You are never out of His sight because He loves you. He knows everything about you, like what you are thinking, how many hairs are on your head, and even what you are going to say. There is nowhere in heaven or earth or the earth below that you can hide from God.

He shaped you, formed you inside and out. He gave you a body, a soul, and a spirit. You are marvelous. He sculpted

46

you from nothing. So if you feel like you are nothing or that you are nobody, you are terribly mistaken. Reread King David's words. They are truth and they are life.

God thinks about you more times than can be counted. He has your name engraved on the palm of His hand. He loves you with an everlasting love. His kind of love is one that we cannot fully understand or comprehend in our minds. A love that is unconditional and undeserved yet freely given to you.

Chapter Insights

As I contemplate my son's experience, I am filled with faith that God loves my son more than I do. The Lord is working everything out for his good. My son is blessed by God because he has accepted Christ Jesus as his Savior.

"God's love"

I am also convinced and filled with faith in God's love for you. That He is working everything out for your good. You are also blessed by God when you accept His Son Jesus Christ as your Lord and Savior too.

If you need to or want to start a new life you can. You can make a decision right now that will change everything. The kind of decision that will cause the old you to become a new creation. You can make a decision to allow your Creator to create a new life for you where your sins are vanished once you confess them, giving you a fresh and new start in life.

A new life begins the moment you make the decision to accept all that Christ offers you.

Hope is instilled into my son's heart now because he chose to secure his future. He is forgiven and given another chance to make things different in his life. This time with help from on High.

Like many people do. Like everyone should. I cried out to God in my darkest hour. Even when they do not believe there is a God they cry out to him in their time of need. He still meets with those who call upon Him where they are.

Call upon Him in your time of need. He will answer you while you are still crying out to Him. He will help you. He will heal you. All you have to do is trust Him.

"God forgives you."

To get a new life simply admit you have sinned (you have done wrong like stealing, lying, adultery, fornicating, harming yourself, cheating, murdering, and all the other types of wrong doing. The Lord already knows everything you have done and He still loves you in spite of them all. He is faithful to forgive you. My son asked the Lord to forgive him and said, "I don't feel like I am in as much trouble now."

When God forgives you He forgets what you have done, He throws it in the depths of the sea. When you repeatedly ask Him to forgive you, like I did for many years, He does not even remember what you are talking about. That is what forgiveness is. It is thorough and it is complete. As it should be when you forgive yourself and when you forgive others. The type of forgiveness our Creator offers cannot be compared to the same type of forgiveness we extend to ourselves or to others for that matter. I have heard the expression, "I will forgive but I will never forget what they did to me!" Well this is partially true. However, one wise woman once told me, "Honey if you are going to bury the hatchet you better bury the handle with it or you will keep tripping over it." Such wise words. When you forgive yourself do it completely. When you forgive others, vow to hold no wrong against them.

"Give yourself a break."

Forgiving yourself means that you no longer hold yourself in debt for the action. You release yourself. You allow the negativity attached to unforgiveness go. If emotions are energy in motion in reality when you let go you are just letting go of negative energy that has been trapped in your soul. Give yourself a break! Forgive yourself! Forgive others. Do it for you. Do it now!

If you are mad at God because you think He is to blame for what has happened to you in life think again. He does not control you does He? I would imagine if He was in control you would be very different than you are now. Nor does He control others.

What happened to you happened because of the choices others have made or that you have made yourself. God gives us all a free will to choose to live right or to live in a way that brings sorrow, heartache and misery not to mention bad health and emotional hell. It is not a hard choice to choose right when you realize you deserve better than what you have right now.

"Change what you believe about yourself and your life will change."

You will attract to you what you have in you. If you are a negative person, thinking bad and feeling bad about yourself you will only attract the type of person that will validate and verify your belief system. Change what you believe about yourself and your life will change.

To find out more about your history and your identity read from one of the most ancient manuscripts in the world. The Holy Bible. Here are a list of Scriptures you can read. They coincide with The Father's Love Letter. You can find it online at www.fathersloveletter.com. It is powerful and transforming. I guarantee you if you watch this video every day for 30 days you will be transformed. You would think differently. Remember you are loved. Created by Love Himself to love and be loved.

(1) Genesis 2:7; (2) Isaiah 64:8; (3) Genesis 2:21-25; (4) Jeremiah 1:4-5; (5) Psalm 139:13; (6) Psalm 71:6; (7) Acts 17:28; (8) Acts 17:26; (9) Genesis 1:27; (10) Romans 8:31-32; (11) Psalm 139:16; (12) Matthew 10:29-31; (13) Jeremiah 31:3; (14) Hebrews 1:14; (15) 1 Peter 5:8; (16) Genesis 3; (17) Ephesians 6:11-12; (18) Romans 5:12; (19) Isaiah 53:6; (20) Acts 17:27; (21) Acts 17:28; (22) Romans 1:21-23; (23) Romans 3:23; (24) 2 Peter 3:9; (25) John 10:10; (26) Revelation 13:8; (27) John 3:16; (28) Philippians 2:5-11; (29) 2 Corinthians 5:21; (30) Colossians 2:13-15; (31) 2 Corinthians 5:18-19; (32) Luke 24; (33) Romans 8:1-2; (34) Hebrews 10:10; (35) John 14:6; (36) Romans 8:15-17; (37) Acts 17:28; (38) Ephesians 1:3-10; (39) 2 Corinthians 5:17; (40) Acts 17:27; (41) John 6:51; (42) 1 Peter 1:3-5; (43) Psalm 8:4-6; (44) Ephesians 2:10, (45) Genesis 1:26; (46) 1 John 4:16; (47) Ephesians 3:14-15; (48) Romans 8:29; (49) John 14:1-3; (50) Galatians 4:4-7; (51) Revelation 21:1-4; (52) Ephesians 1:11-23; (53) John 1:12-13 (54) Hebrews 2:9-11; (55) Romans 8:19 (56) Romans 10:9

6

MY BROTHER HUNG HIMSELF
ON EASTER MORNING

My step-brother had some issues that were never dealt
with, reconciled or resolved. (Sounds like a familiar story
about my friend who shot himself doesn't it?). My brother
was also experiencing some anguish, some distress, some
grief, and some depression because his wife left him and
took their young daughter back to Germany with her. He
was a great dad. Just not a great husband in his wife's
opinion. He was devastated. He started drinking heavily,
took illegal drugs and tried to relieve the pain any way he
knew how. It was not enough. The pain never subsided.
He never stopped trying to drown the pain either.

He came to East Texas where we lived and seemed to be
getting his life together and doing good. He started going
to church and finding peace and purpose for his life. Until
one "well-meaning" church woman told him he had a

demon in him. If she was not going to cast the demon out why did she even say anything? Folks, let me tell you, this is not something you accuse someone of unless you are a mature Christian and are willing to work with the person you discern has a demon.

He knew about his demons. He had been into some serious dark stuff like necromancy. He was all too familiar with the dark side. He needed help. He wanted help. He never got the help he needed or wanted. The person who was so eager and willing to point out his problems was never willing to help him or even let him know where he could get help. Don't every tell anyone something like that unless you personally are ready to help them get freedom or know someone who can help them. It is dangerous. Looking back on his life, it was at that point it changed.

It was the turning point for him. He decided if he had a devil in him he would just start living like the devil. It was not a quick process, it was not immediate, but his actions let us all see those unspoken words as he played out one risky scene after another.

He finally went for professional help and was diagnosed as paranoid schizophrenic. He was given medication. As most people who are experiencing internal wounds he took his medication and he continued to drink profusely. This is never a good combination. As most self-abusers would agree, anything to dull the pain is better than nothing.

"He hung himself on Easter morning."

He and his friend were drinking heavily and only the Lord knows what else he was taking. His friend left the apartment to get some more alcohol. They had been working on making a hangman's nooce. When his friend left, my brother went to the balcony of the second story apartment complex, tied the rope off to the railing, put the noose around his neck and jumped. He hung himself on Easter morning.

We were out of town visiting another church. They called the church phone and the pastor answered. I knew he looked different, strange, and a little pale when he came back to his seat. I knew he has received some bad news.

He sat down in his seat in front of mine, turned around and looked me in the eyes. My throat dried up, I got sick to my stomach, I knew something bad had happened and I did not want to hear what it was. I wanted to spare myself the pain I knew I was going to feel as soon as he spoke. Time stood still for me. My breath was shallow and bated as I sat there, wanting to know what was said and not wanting to know what was said all at the same time.

"He is dead."

He turned and spoke in a very soft, concerned voice, "Cindy that was your mother who called. They just found your brother. He has hung himself. He is dead."

Words you never expect to hear in church. Your brother is dead. He hung himself. How do you get that out of your head? Out of your heart? How do you process that information? What do you do with the pain that stabbed your heart like a dagger in that moment?

I weep now as I write this chapter. I can only share my part of the story. I can only imagine how his daughter must have felt when she heard the words, "your daddy is dead." I can only imagine how his mother felt as she was told that her son took his life. I cannot express how his three brothers felt when they learned of his tragic death.

How did his other (step) parents feel? They had been in his life since he was a small boy.

"The comfort of the Holy Spirit engulfed me."

I can say I am grateful I was in church, even if we were far from home, when I received this news. The pastor stopped the service. He called my husband and I up to the altar. He expressed his heartfelt condolences to us. Then he led everyone in the church in prayer for us and our family. At some point I found myself out on the floor covered with the prayer shawl my Messianic Jewish minister was wearing.

The comfort of the Holy Spirit engulfed me. I felt an indescribable peace come upon my broken and grieving heart. The Lord touched me profoundly and deeply that day. Although the questions still remained in my mind and the tears still spilled out of my eyes, the intense pain I felt from the loss was soothed. We stayed in church that day and finished out the service.

The aftermath of his death was dreadful. Going through my brother's belongings, calling family members and hearing them cry and scream over the phone was such a hard thing to do. Planning the memorial service after his cremation was hard. The plans that had to be made were not expected and therefore left us all unsure of what he would have wanted so we just had to do our best by having a memorial for him. His dad held his picture at the memorial service and wept bitterly over the loss of his son. Everyone was affected by his premature passing and short-lived life.

Chapter Insights

If you think no one cares about you think again. If you think you will not be missed think again. If you think you have no purpose in life think again. You are loved. People will miss you. You have a powerful impact on the lives of others even if you don't think you do. You have a purpose for living. If you do not know what it is find someone to help you discover it or unpack it with you.

"Wasn't there something I could have done?"

How do you not ask yourself this one question when something like this happens: Wasn't there something I could have done?

Then other questions like these: There must have been something I could have said that could have made a difference? And then of course, there is the "How did I not know he was hurting that bad?" question that many people ask themselves and others.

These questions and hundreds of others pommel our brains while the pain of the loss batters our hearts. Those of us who have experienced the death of a loved one because they choose to take their life have a unique set of circumstances to contend with. A traumatic and tragic death is more devastating than other types of death.

At his memorial service I knelt at the feet of my step-brother's mother and loved on her, told her how sorry I was, and how much my heart was breaking for her. I tried to comfort her but really I knew there were no words to speak that would or could ever comfort this mother's distraught heart.

To this day I am still impacted by my brother's death. I am not sure I will ever get over it completely. How can you? It was so shocking. I had never experienced anything in my life as shocking and as painful as this was. I do not think about this event as often as I once did. The pain has subsided, but as writing this book just proved, there is still tenderness and pain in my heart because of it. I still miss him. I know everyone that knew him still misses him. He was an awesome guy.

I know you still miss your loved one too. I am sorry for your loss. I pray your find peace and healing in your heart as I have. Your loss is great and at times the pain can seem to be unbearable. There are others who understand your pain all too well.

If you are reading this book I know you have been impacted by someone in your life or perhaps you have been personally impacted because you have tried to harm yourself, or even commit suicide. I know it is not easy to survive the loss of a wounded soul whether they be a spouse, brother, sister, mother, father, friend or coworker. They leave an empty spot in your life that no one else can or ever will fill.

So how do we, those of us who have been left behind, find peace, make peace, receive peace where there is nothing but pain?

"We must feel the pain."

First of all, we must feel the pain. We must embrace the sorrow, the grief, the anger, whatever emotion we are experiencing at the time. We must feel the pain if we are ever going to find peace or healing for our wounds over their death. Stuffing the pain of the loss never accomplishes anything. It only complicates things for you.

Internal wounds fester and came become "infected" just like external wounds. The 'source' or the root of the wound must be dealt with and removed for true healing to happen. One of the ways to begin removing the 'source' or the splinter is to forgive. We can forgive the person who took their life, or harmed themselves. We must forgive them. If you harmed yourself then you must find a way to forgive yourself for the things you blame yourself for and you need to forgive yourself for hurting yourself.

We must also understand that we cannot blame ourselves for what others choose to do. It was not our fault. We cannot blame ourselves and get caught up in a cycle of blame and despair. If you are convinced someone's death was caused by your actions, that it was your fault for some real and legitimate reason, you still do not have enough power over another person to make them take their own life. For example if you broke up with someone you were dating, or divorced them, they may be wounded and angry, but you did not cause them to do what they did if they took their life. They did what they did as a result of their own way of processing the circumstance or not. They did it because of the internal wounds they had that never healed. Perhaps they even did it to get back at you. It still does not mean you have control over them to cause them to harm themselves.

You must find a way to make peace within yourself. You can get help by talking to someone. You can join a grief or a survivor's support group. They are helpful and they keep you from being isolated. Isolation is a not good for anyone. Try your best not to isolate.

I still miss my brother. I know his mother and his other siblings still miss him. What about his daughter? Do you think he was thinking about anyone at the time? Or perhaps he was thinking about every one and decided that we would all be better off without him. I tell you we are not! No one is ever better off because you take your life.

That is a lie. If you are thinking of taking your life please think of those you will be leaving behind. Their lives will not be the same without you. Your life does matter. You are important and you have a destiny.

7

I'M GLAD I "FAILED"
author chooses to remain anonymous
This testimony is unedited and quoted as it was written

From the beginning: I'm a female, live in a pretty rural setting, was 20 years old when things got really bad. I've experienced complex trauma and was pretty angry, violent, self-destructive, depressed etc., all through childhood and adolescence. I moved to a new town in my late teens, got a job at a local social services agency, and moved into an apartment, which after about 9 months my partner moved into also. Mid December — right before finals week at college, actually — my partner and I ended things and she moved out. We had been together the while time I had lived in that new town, and so suddenly I had:

1) Significantly fewer social ties

2) Significantly more time to spend alone

and 3) All of the same trauma junk that had driven me to self-destruction over and over and over again, ad museum, over the course of my life to date.

"I was passively suicidal…"

I stopped eating. Over the course of that spring, I lost almost a quarter of my body weight. I was passively suicidal, but I had been passively suicidal for years at a time with only intermittent breaks. I was dissociating a lot, and isolating, but again, I had seen those before. I was still working and going to college pretty consistently up until the end of March. But by April, a couple new symptoms had popped up. For starters, I was drinking every weekend, and sometimes during the week, and drinking to the point of impairment. This isn't unusual for most 20-year-olds, but I had probably only consumed alcohol 4 or 5 times in my life prior to that month. I was smoking weed every night after work. Again, not necessarily generally unusual, but to me, yes. It also wasn't helping, either, only making me more depressed, paralyzed, and paranoid.

"Which brings me to paranoia."

Which brings me to paranoia. The last few weeks before the s*** hit the fan, I didn't trust anyone. I had a close friend come over to watch movies and I was convinced he hated me and was currently texting people bad things about me. I kept my blinds shut because I was scared of my neighbors, and I knew if I had them open, they would be peering in.

I was also crying all the time. One day, I cried for probably 3 or 4 hours straight, took a break, and cried for another 3-4 hour stretch. I remember trying to leave my house to get a burger and making it only to my front steps before sitting down and bursting into tears again. And I wasn't going to school. I dropped all my coursework two weeks before finals. Somehow, I passed all but one of my classes. I was still going to work up until I was hospitalized.

So, hospital. I go in one weekend for an emergency counseling session. On-call counselor suggests I go to the ER. ER thoroughly quizzes me about my intent to harm myself and sends me home with Ativan and a doctor's appointment for the next morning. The next week, I break down and tell my therapist I've been seriously considering taking all the pills in my medicine cabinet. By Friday, I am admitted to the hospital for suicidal ideation. I stay there a week, go home. Two weeks later, I'm back. This time I got the pills all ready, I have the booze to take them with, I've taken a few shots to build up courage, but I got scared and walked myself (barefoot, tipsy) to the ER. Admitted. Hospitalized, take 2.

"Death freaks me out."

Obviously, I'm pretty ambivalent about dying at that point. I wanted to, but I was also afraid. Since I was a little girl, I've been massively and unusually aware of mortality. Death freaks me out. But my life is getting worse at this point. I quit my job. I relocate to an actual city with more outpatient resources and some new faces — people who don't know me as "the smiling friendly young girl who works at [insert social services agency here]". What is supposed to be a fresh start turns into a nightmare. If you ever consider moving spontaneously in the midst of a mental health crisis... don't. It is a bad idea. The fact that I thought it was smart is only tribute to how unwell I was at the time.

So I'm in the city. I have a couple more hospital stays.

I've started taking my prescribed meds in seemingly random combinations. They're non-lethal doses, and I'm not taking them to get recreationally high; I'm literally just taking them to f*** with my body and hurt myself. I used to cut my arms back in my early teens, but this seems like an even form of self-injury. The best part is, afterwards I feel really weak and tired and sleep for a while. It's the escape I always sought with cutting, but without the sharp pain or the blood or the risk of getting caught.

(THIS WAS THE WAY MY SICK BRAIN THOUGHT. I do NOT endorse self-injurious overdosing. The "weakness" and "sleepiness" was, of course, my body literally working out poison. Luckily, my liver ended up fine, but had I continued on this route for much longer, I could have done long-term or even short-term fatal damage to my organs — EVEN ACCIDENTALLY, EVEN WHEN I WAS "ONLY" SELF HARMING.)

"…every moment of every day is consumed with trying to escape the traumatic memories…"

By now, I'm alienated from a lot of people in my life, and those who I'm not alienated from, live very far away. I'm in a strange city when I have only lived in very small towns previously, I'm unemployed with no prospects, I'm very close to being homeless, I'm on food stamps (which was a huge blow to me at the time because I was very set on never needing to use government benefits), and every moment of every day is consumed with trying to escape the traumatic memories which keep flooding my brain.

Of course, the more I fight them, the more they propagate. I was acting erratic. I was acting weird. I had lost everything — home, job, relationship, friends — in the span of 6-7 months. I felt I had no options, nowhere to go. Furthermore, I was in the midst of an existential crisis that had convinced me all the goals and aspirations I had ever had in my life thus far had been meaningless and pointless wastes of time and breath.

I took too many Tylenol. How many doesn't matter — the dose had potential for lethality, is all I'll say. It was the second time I had overdosed on that particular drug that week. The circumstances were complicated. I had just gotten released from the ER, where my outpatient program had brought me under concern I would overdose. After trying to dip out on the guards assigned to me in the waiting room for a while, I convinced the ER doc I was fine to go and he sent me home with instructions to "come back if it got worse again".

"...found a semi-private grassy spot to sit, and prepared to overdose."

Earlier in the day, I had called my therapist from back home, who I was still in contact with, and gotten voicemail. Just wanted to check in with her. She returned the call as I was walking out of the Emergency Room. We were on the phone talking as I retrieved my water bottle from the outpatient clinic, found a semi-private grassy spot to sit, and prepared to overdose. I was pretty despondent, pretty apathetic, and at the end of our conversation she asked if I could agree to stay safe until we spoke again. I was honest and again, still afraid of death on a very basic level, and told her I didn't even feel safe then.

She told me she was sorry but she had to call 911. I swallowed the pills, hoping they would do something before paramedics came, especially since they didn't know exactly where I was. I laid down, watched the sky, waited for the pills to work. (At that time, I wasn't very aware of the exact mechanism Tylenol overdose would use to kill. I didn't know it would take days for me to die and that I probably wouldn't even be sick for about 24 hours.)

TURNS OUT, I had taken Tylenol PM unknowingly, which is probably a big reason I am still okay. I think that, if I didn't feel sick from the meds after half an hour, I would probably have gotten flighty and ran, making it even harder for anyone to find me. I probably would have taken more pills as I was leaving, making me more sick. I know myself and how impulsive I was at the time, and how my "ambivalence" about death was quickly being overtaken by my irrational impulsivity. But as was, after maybe 20 minutes I was feeling very sick. Nauseous, like I expected, but I couldn't sit up well, or stand up at all. My depth perception was all messed up. Everything felt heavy. I felt loopy, disoriented, and generally terrible.

Kay Redfield Jamison writes in her memoir, in the section about her suicidal overdose, about how a drugged mind operates differently than a sober mind. Like I said, my sober mind probably would have "fled the scene". My drugged mind, turned around by the massive dose of Benadryl I had accidentally consumed, freaked out, embraced ambivalence, and called 911 herself. Go drugged mind.

"I'm admitted to the psych ward, thoroughly shaken up and upset..."

After about an hour, cops show up. Paramedics show up. They help me to the ambulance. I barf in the ambulance, right as they strap me on the stretcher. (It doesn't make since for nauseous, pukey people to ride backwards and strapped down at the shoulders, does it?!?) By the time I'm in the ER, I'm tripping out. I keep "losing time", I remember touching my leg over and over because I was amazed at how it didn't feel like my leg. They order blood work. My Tylenol levels are really high at first; they go down enough without the antidote, though, that I don't need it. I'm admitted to the psych ward, thoroughly shaken up and upset, but healthy enough.

"[I] …have no desire to kill myself."

I wish I could say that was the end of it. I had a few more overdoses, and I tried to hang myself while at treatment (the staff intervened.) Treatment: I went to a residential treatment program for nine months. It was secure, a lockdown, the kind of place where they can assign a staff member to keep arms-length distance from you at all times to make sure you're safe. It sucked and was hard to do but ultimately, it worked, because: I'm out now, fully on my own again, and have no desire to kill myself.

Sometimes, I want to overdose as a self-injurious thing… But I don't, because I remember how grateful I am that my liver is fine and that I really do want to keep it that way.

Sometimes, I still want to self-harm by cutting. Honestly, it's 1:30 AM as I write this and I'm mostly writing it to distract myself from the huge urge to take my pencil sharpener to my leg. HOWEVER, I am distracting, and am so far successfully safe, so that's a win so far.

"Life is okay now. It's not great, but it's better."

If I had died last summer, there would have been a lot of things I would have missed. Life is okay now. It's not great, but it's better. Everything hurts a little less, less of the time.

I just started a job I really enjoy, my family relationships are good, I see friends often. I have hobbies, like writing and walking. Yeah, stuff is still hard. The trauma hasn't magically evaporated yet (I'm told that it never will.) But I'm also not wandering aimlessly in stripper heels around sketchy neighborhoods, trying to run it out of me. I'm not poisoning it out. I'm not trying to kill it. I'm working with it. Most days, I can still hardly even name out loud what happened to me. But I'm trying.

If I could give one piece of advice to a suicidal person, it would be to ask themselves what it is they really want or need. I think there are some suicidal people who truly, honestly, just plain want to die, no matter what. But I also think there are a lot of people, like me, who are ambivalent about death but who also have problems they just can't solve.

"I wanted those pieces of pain to go away, or to get better."

For me, it was the complex trauma, the existential hopelessness, and the lack of options. I didn't want to die; I wanted those pieces of pain to go away, or to get better. It turns out with some therapy, spiritual connection, and counseling around different options and referrals, I've done okay. I solved the problem enough that it's not unbearable anymore.

"I'm glad I didn't die."

Today, I'm glad I'm alive. I'm glad I didn't die. I'm glad I "failed", and I honestly believe that you — if you're suicidal — can get to this point too. (ariii, 2015)

Chapter Insights

This young woman struggled with many things. She was traumatized. What kind of trauma this young woman experienced does not matter. What matters is that she obviously never dealt with the trauma she experienced.

She internalized it. She stuffed it. She tried to go on with life with a wounded soul. Listen to her description, "I was pretty angry, violent, self-destructive and depressed" (Anonymous). Why? Because she was wounded.

Now listen to me, do not be like this young woman. Depression is only anger turned inside. Anger is a symptom of helplessness and frustration. Hope deferred makes the heart sick. (Proverbs 13:12). Our internalized or emotional pain can make us both mentally and physically sick.

Merle Shain (1985), says it so eloquently,

> …because despair is anger with no place to go, pain that has gone inside and dug in deep, and because the body and the mind are not two separate things but only one, the mind's pain usually shows up somewhere else, so the search for self is a search for health (p. 30, para 3).

What would have happened had she asked for help, had she turned to a school counselor, talked to a friend, went to a pastor? The community is full of people in the people helping profession. There are crisis hotlines and all types of websites where people are waiting to help you. There is no reason to continue internalizing what happened to you and isolate yourself from everyone because of what was done to you. Be brave. Take the first step. Reach out to someone you can trust. Tell them your story.

"Do not stay angry and self-destructive."

You have a voice. If you are abused you still have a voice whether you think you do or not. Use your voice and get some help. Reach out. Do not stay angry and self-destructive. Find a way to tell your story. Write it down.

Write a book. Send an article to a magazine. Just do something. Release the pain inside of you. Find a way.

Why was the young woman in this testimony so self-destructive? From what I see in her story after she experienced the complex trauma she began to see herself differently. She exhibits signs of self-hatred, and self-loathing. With those came the self-harming behaviors because of her beliefs about herself that developed from her traumatic event.

Did you catch it when she said she was drinking and smoking marijuana, and it was not helping? She said it was actually, "making me more depressed, paralyzed, and paranoid." Drugs and alcohol may provide a temporary nulling or numbing effect but they are not solutions. These forms of escape only cause more problems. They are not solutions.

We need to be solution oriented not focused on the problems. If you want a different life, if you want a life that is happy, peaceful, and successful, you must change the way you think about you and the rest of the people in your life. Then put your faith in something besides a pill, a bottle of alcohol, or a weed.

"One event in your life can change you forever."

One event in your life can change you forever. There may have been other traumatic events in her life as a child. There are usually all kinds of abuse we experience as children, even if we have great parents. How we cope with them is what makes the difference. Learning to develop some good coping skills is vital to surviving all the abuse, trauma, and even all the self-inflicted pain. You can learn anything you need to help your life become richer and abundant life.

Please understand that I am no minimalizing your pain or the events in your life that left you wounded. I know I had wounds I had to work through. I got the help I needed to get the healing I needed. What my heart is trying to do through this book is to get your to see past your pain into your future.

Learn some coping skills like how to forgive others and your self. Learn some conflict resolution skills. Learn how to set some healthy boundaries. Unfortunately, we did not come with a manual to know how to do things or how to cope with things that happen or that are happening to us throughout life. We do have the Word of God that can guide us through all types of situations. Everything we need can be found within it's pages.

I would like to' recommend a website I found during my research for this book. Have I Got a Problem. This website provides free online counseling. You can also visit this website and read or download for free coping skills. http://www.haveigotaproblem.com/download/ 191/How-To-Improve-Coping-Skills. Put some coping skills into practice. Your life will begin to get better. You will be glad you did.

Other suggested readings:

Making Peace With Your Past: One Choice At A Time by Cindy Hyde

Boundaries by Cloud and Townsend

Both books are available online at www.Amazon.com

8

A MASSIVE WEIGHT LIFTED
author chooses to remain anonymous
This testimony is unedited and quoted as it was written

I think things have gotten better for me. *Extremely* better, and all in the course of 24 hours. That's right.... just *one day*. Basically I told someone that I was planning to kill myself and right after that I felt a massive weight was lifted off my shoulders.

"I will not be contemplating suicide again anytime soon."

I've been able to control my overthinking more in the past few hours than I ever have before (I'm actually starting to realize when I overthink!), and I can also tell that I will not be contemplating suicide again anytime soon.

"I've never felt so good in my life"

I've never felt so good in my life, and I feel like things are finally looking up and changing for the better. I will continue to see my therapist just to make sure things are OK now and again, but I think after I finally told someone how bad I was feeling that the worst ended in that very moment.

I have been battling suicide seriously for a few months now, and I think it is finally over. I'm happy I chose to stay. I really am.

"I believe in you. You can do it. You are strong."

As for those that are reading this and are still battling, keep fighting. I believe in you. You can do it. You are strong. And, most importantly, you are loved. I love you all.

"...you are loved."

Chapter Insights

I was amazed at how quickly things turned around for this person. In just 24 hours they went from being suicidal to being "extremely better" This has happened to them. It is their reality. This can happen for you too. In fact, it happens more often than you think.

Do you realize what happened to make this person feel better? They simply talked to someone. You may not think that talking to someone is a big deal but it is. Isolation is a tool the enemy of your soul uses to keep you from connecting with others because if you actually connect... what could happen? Just what happened in this testimony. Healing, freedom, deliverance, whatever you want to call it.

When you isolate yourself and your mind is not in a healthy place, you can think all types of irrational thoughts. They may sound right at the time but once you give voice to that which is causing you anguish, misery, pain or turmoil in your life you hear what you are saying yourself and it often causes your mind to find solutions, relieve the anguish and yes, even ease the pain.

"Opening yourself up to expose the dark and deep secrets of your mind brings you freedom."

Talking things over with someone requires you to feel safe. It needs to be someone you trust or someone like a therapist, a pastor or minister, a friend you know will be there for you and with you through it all. Opening yourself up to expose the dark and deep secrets of your mind brings you freedom. It just does.

I have many hurting people come in my office. Many of them just need to be heard. That's right. They just need to know someone will hear them, really listen to them. They need to tell their story. They need to feel like someone cares about them enough to listen to them. I mostly listen to whatever it is they have to say. Often, through tears and sobs and between the multiple tissues, they open up and divulge the real source of their pain.

"There is something about getting it out that makes the difference."

As they tell their story, or parts of it, they begin to cry less. The tears begin to slow down. Their breathing is not as labored and shallow. Their countenance begins to change. All because they released the story, the source of pain. They got it out of them. There is something about getting it out that makes a big difference.

This is the analogy I frequently use. The Lord gave me the

visual many years ago. I love it when He does that and when He uses the practical things of this world to reveal spiritual truths to us.

When you get a splinter in your finger it hurts. This symbolizes words or actions that stick into your soul or your heart. If the splinter is not removed it begins to remove itself. It turns red, gets swollen, hurts even more, and eventually if it is in the finger long enough will get infected. If the splinter is removed, it will heal. But as long as the splinter is in there it will not. If the splinter represents the words or the traumatic event that is in your heart, mind, or soul, then to heal it must be removed and the wound will then heal. Otherwise it will not.

I know this is a simple analogy but it is so true. Leave the source of the pain inside of you and it will continue to be the thing you focus your attention and energy on. And what happens when you have a sore finger from a splinter? You hit your finger and hurt it even more. You are constantly thinking about your finger because of the continual pain right? Same thing happens internally when we are wounded.

"...he really didn't want to feel what he was feeling anymore"

I ministered to a young man once. He had some issues he was working through. I listened to his story. He explained why he was feeling the way he was. I asked him a few questions about his feelings and within a very few minutes he realized he really didn't want to feel what he was feeling anymore. After a few more pointed and anointed questions he came up with some pretty good solutions to his problems. Most people do. If they are given the opportunity to explore their options from a different perspective they will come up with solutions. So can you. Your mind and your spirit will actually give you some answers and some solutions to some of the problems you face, and that will help you relieve some of the pain you carry around inside of you. You do not have to stay wounded. You can help yourself by getting some help.

The human brain is amazing. The human spirit is even more amazing! He also said he felt a weight lift. In fact, he actually said he felt like a football player had been lifted off his chest. He felt so free and so peaceful afterwards.

9

COMPLETE
author chooses to remain anonymous
This testimony is unedited and quoted as it was written

This message is for those of you who are thinking about suicide.

Like you, I did not really want to kill myself. I just wanted the overwhelming pain to stop. It felt like I was having a 24 hour anxiety attack. I could not concentrate. I was obsessing on fearful thoughts and feelings. My adrenalin was so high it felt like my blood was boiling. I felt I had to do something impulsive to stop the pain. I was going through a nervous breakdown. I was feeling frantic, fearful, overwhelmed, and angry all at the same time. It felt like I was losing my mind. I was feeling guilty, ashamed and like a failure for having these thoughts and feelings.

Being desperate for help, I called Suicide Prevention and the crisis line so much they always had to tell me I had reached my call limit for the day. A counselor told me to go within myself to feel better. All I felt was empty inside and this made me feel more alone. Then I thought God was punishing me for something stupid I did in the past. Even though I do not believe in reincarnation, I prayed for this life and any past lives for forgiveness of any wrongdoing I did. (I just wanted to cover all my bases.) It did not work.

"God is there with us, and in us, when we go through hard times."

I found out later, God does not work that way. God does not punish people by giving them overwhelming experiences to teach them a lesson. God is there with us, and in us, when we go through hard times. God also forgives us before we ask. When we ask for forgiveness it is not for God, but for us, to reconnect with God who never loved us any less when we made mistakes. Sometimes we think we disappointed God and we feel unworthy of anything good in life because we think God holds a grudge against us. We lose our connection with God out of our fear. This is the best time to talk to God because we know for a fact that God is listening. Sometimes you will get answers. Have you ever had a wonderful idea, but you did not think of it? That's our creator blessing us with wisdom.

At that time I was so mad at God for not answering me the way I wanted him to. I would say, "Come on God! Would you hurry up here! I've haven't got all day!!" Then I would yell and curse at God. "How dare you leave me unloved, unprotected and in pain!" There was no lightning bolt that hit me. Nothing bad happened to me either. The creator of the universe was able to take my rudeness and tantrums and love me anyway. God did answer me, and my problems did come to pass, but not the way I thought they would. God was much more creative than I was.

Things turned out very well.

Good to know.

I had well-meaning people try to help me through the suicidal thoughts and feelings. For anyone who is trying to help someone through this experience, please say you care for them, you love them, you are there for them, you are listening to them, and together you will find help.

I had some pretty inappropriate things said to me when I was suicidal. These remarks made me feel more alone, ignored and much worse. I am wondering if you heard any of these comments.

"Just pull yourself up and out of it."

"Stop feeling sorry for yourself."

"Well, you should have done this instead of what you did."

"Remember, there is always someone who has it worse than you do."

Have you ever seen someone being tortured to death? Could you imagine someone going on and saying these things to that person?

Not only would the person not be able to hear you (because they have other things on their mind) but they wouldn't have the strength to flip them off. If you could pull yourself up and out of it you would have done so already. There are people in the world worse off than us, but that is not the issue. The issue is that you are feeling like hell right now and need help.

"I tried to kill myself 7 times."

I tried to kill myself 7 times. I was accused of being selfish and not thinking of my loved ones. Getting back to that person being tortured or people who killed themselves in concentration camps, were they thinking, "Gee I wonder how my friends and family are doing right now?" Nobody was being selfish. They just wanted the pain to stop. I understand this. I remember someone telling me I was going to go to hell for all eternity if I killed myself. Does anyone really think God, the author of unconditional love, the creator of this universe, actually sends all those poor people to hell? God did not send me to hell when I killed myself for a few minutes during one of my suicide attempts. I did not go to hell. I went to a place of love, light, and knowledge.

"I went to a place of love, light, and knowledge."

At the same time, we both know God does not want you to kill yourself. God and other people in the world want you to give yourself some time to get better. I've noticed one of the main reasons some people get suicidal is because of what someone thinks about them. Whether a person is being bullied at school, lost their girl/boyfriend, split up with their wife/husband, people at your job giving you a bad time, or no job or financial relief in sight, someone or a pet died and you do not have a strong support system in your life, if you are gay and feeling all alone and suicide feels like the only way out, remember things always change. That is the only thing in life we can count on. This too shall pass.

You need to protect yourself from other people's opinions right now. Don't let their thoughts become your reality. People always have their ideas, but that does not make them right. I had no sense of myself growing up. Whatever anyone said to me I believed! I thought they were saying God's honest truth. I was just like a sponge, soaking up everyone's thoughts and opinions about me. I had no idea that I had a right to my opinion about myself. It is your birthright. Once I learned this it was really easy to weed out the truth about myself and let go of other people's remarks.

"This too shall pass."

I was hospitalized and the medication back then was not working. I lost my spouse (who had me served with divorce papers in the hospital on my birthday), my job, my apartment, my friends, and my mind. My mother was also diagnosed with breast cancer and I lost my father to colon cancer a few years earlier. I was getting worse and my body was shaking so badly I would choke on food while I was eating.

The psychiatrist (who was weirder than I'll ever be) said I had a strong suicidal drive. Who wouldn't have a strong suicidal drive after trying it 7 times? He decided I needed to be put in a straightjacket and sit at the nurses' station all day. I was transferred to a different hospital to get E.C.T. (electroconvulsive therapy). I remember entering the other hospital. The paramedic rolling me in on a gurney and me wearing (you guessed it) my little white straightjacket. The staff and patients were scared of me at first. One nurse looked right at me and said, "UH-OH." Once they realized I was not Hannibal Lector, they took me out of the straightjacket. Now able to move around, I went outside on the patio. I thought, "I can't believe I am going to have E.C.T."

Even though I lost everything including my mind, I had nothing left, and there was nothing left of me, I felt something in my gut. It was so tiny, yet so strong and grounding. I wondered what that was. I found out later it was my soul. The place where God is inside us. Our soul is immortal, perfect, whole and complete. We all have one. Our soul never changes no matter what we do in life. God is inside us every step of the way.

"God is inside us every step of the way."

The good news is that was 23 years ago. I made it and you will too. Please be kind and patient with yourself. If you knew someone feeling suicidal, what would you say to them? You would probably tell them the same thing I am telling you. KNOW that you are worth living and God loves us ALL. No matter what you heard, no matter what society says. God and people in the world love you too.

If someone feels otherwise, that is their issue, not yours. If you can't think of anyone who loves you right now, know you just have not met them yet. Please be patient, kind and gentle with yourself during this tender time by not putting yourself down. Remember that you are a good person going through a horrible time, not a horrible person going through a good time. I used to put myself down and it just made the healing process harder and longer.

More good news is that there are a lot more medications that work more effectively now and good therapists than there were over 20 years ago. Now fewer people have to have E.C.T. like I did. If you are one of the few that has to have E.C.T. the doctors have improved on it as well. Just ask Carrie Fisher.

At first what helped me was the E.C.T. Next was the right medications and therapy. They have found out this combination does work the best. This does take a little time, but you are worth every minute of it. I also wanted to tell you, trust the process of therapy. It may take a few sessions for you to build up trust with the therapist, and you need to stay alive when in therapy so you can get rid of the pain.

There are support groups such as Divorce recovery, Grief support, Depression and Anxiety and NAMI (National Alliance for the Mentally Ill). You can also call Suicide Prevention and the crisis line (as long as you don't call them 100 times a day like I did!)

Another thing that is really helpful is to write down your thoughts and feelings. This gets the emotion out on paper and your mind becomes clear.

A nurse told me instead of worrying all night, go to sleep, because when you are sleeping your subconscious can work things out. Plus, your body needs the extra rest from being drained out.

"You are going to be amazed what God has in store for you."

I also found comfort in going to a safe place to worship. I appreciate the small things in life much more now. Like when you're driving and all the lights turn green, putting on warm clothes that just came out of the dryer, when a checkout line opens up and you do not have to wait. I also love to see dogs in the back of cars and trucks just wagging their tails so fast, drinking clean water, staying somewhere safe and dry. All this is here for you to enjoy and you deserve it all and so much more. You are going to be so proud of yourself. You are going to be amazed what God has in store for you. I promise.

10

YOU ARE ALIVE FOR A REASON
SO DON'T EVER GIVE UP
author chooses to remain anonymous
This testimony is unedited and quoted as it was written

When you feel like giving up, just remember the reason why you held on for so long

I'm here for the same reason most everyone is, I've given up and I thought suicide was the only way out. Just a few days ago I posted something, but since then I've done some thinking. If suicide is the only way to find peace, then why have we held on for so long? It's not because we love the pain we are in, it's because one day we hope we wake up and hope the world will treat us better.

It might also be because we know if we go we will be hurting our friends and family. Things may never get much better, but you'll never know. I know things seem bad now, and I know having depression doesn't help the situation, but you will get through it. You might not know me, and I might not know you, but together we will face this.

You are loved; you might not see it now.

Any scars (physical, mental or emotional) you have use them as a reminder that you lived.

"Place your hand over your heart, can you feel it? That is called purpose. You're alive for a reason so don't ever give up." -Unknown

Chapter Insights

I am so thankful to hear testimonies like this that are so encouraging to those who may be depressed and contemplating hurting themselves. If that is you... Please don't hurt yourself.

Don't you think you are hurting enough already? Isn't what you are looking for is a better way to live, a more peaceful life, a life that is not focused on the pain of the past?

Let me provide you with some information in this chapter that may help you even more. The author of this chapter says, "Place your hand over your heart, can you feel it? That is called purpose. You're alive for a reason so don't ever give up."

"Don't ever give up"

They are right. Don't ever give up. You are here for a purpose. You were created on purpose for a purpose. Would you like to know why you were created?

First of all you are God's masterpiece. You are created to do amazing works. You were created to live for eternity. "You are not a mistake, or the result of some random, impersonal, mathematically impossible, biological uncertainty (whywewerecreated.com, 2013).

The real truth of the matter is that you are an "image bearer of Almighty God" (whywewerecreated.com, 2013).

You are created by Love to love and be loved. The Ancient text states "God is love." I John 4:8.

> "This is how much God loved the world: He gave his Son, his one and only Son. And this is why: so that no one need be destroyed; by believing in him, anyone can have a whole and lasting life. God didn't go to all the trouble of sending his Son merely to point an accusing finger, telling the world how bad it was. He came to help, to put the world right again. Anyone who trusts in him is acquitted; anyone who refuses to trust him has long since been under the death sentence without knowing it. And why? Because of that person's failure to believe in the one-of-a-kind Son of God when introduced to him." John 3:16-18 MSG

11

VICTORIOUS GRACE
Kim's Story

I was raised in a dysfunctional family. I never really had a father figure. My father left when I was three months old. The father figures I did have in my life sexually abused me.

I had been sexually abused by my step-father, step-brother, other family members as well as other men who were around me. Every man in my life caused me nothing but pain.

As a child I remember my mom trying to commit suicide several times. She almost succeeded. As a way out from pain, suicide seemed to be an option for me. It was usually triggered whenever I would go through a crisis with a boyfriend or some male figure in my life.

I had tried to commit suicide about four times between the ages of 11 and 14. Then again when I was 19. The last time was when I was 20.

Whenever I was thinking about suicide it was usually because I wanted to stop the pain.

I had gotten in a very abusive relationship. He was really bad. He would beat me until I was unrecognizable. He choked me unconscious once. When I came to he had taken a bunch of pills and told me I had to take them too and chase them down with whiskey. The phone rang and I was conscious enough to answer it. The next thing I know I was waking up in the hospital emergency room. They were pumping my stomach. I remember hearing them say, "She has enough in her to kill an elephant." I was in and out of consciousness for a while. I survived that ordeal.

About a year of trying to get away from him, him hunting me down, threating to burn my house down, me knowing he meant it and that he would do what he said I was really nervous and frightened for my life. The guy I was with was so evil and so mean that after all the abuse I endured I decided that the literal hell would be better than this hell I was in. Suicide was my only way out.

"God are you real?"

I took my children to a babysitter. I gathered their teddy bears, a candle, all kinds of pills, (enough to make sure they would kill me) and I went to my living room. I sat the bears in a chair, lit the candle and took the pills. That was when I said, "God are you real?"

"If you are real then don't let me die. If you're not then never mind."

I passed out. The next morning I woke up. And I was amazed. I could not believe I was still alive. And I could not believe I was not even sick. No side effects from overdosing on all those pills. Oh my God I'm alive. Am I dreaming? I went to the cabinet to check and see if I really took all those pills and I had. I was thinking how could that be that I am not even sick.

My son's kindergartner teacher called about my son's struggling in school. The time I woke up for a conference. I went to the conference with her and she led me to Christ. Even driving there I kept thinking, "I'm not even sick." I was just in amazement.

Whenever I was talking to her I saw Jesus in her eyes. For the first time in my life I actually saw the love of Jesus and it was in her eyes. I felt love. I could not get it off of my mind.

"I want to hear more about Jesus."

After a few days I called her. After talking to her for a minute about my son I said, "I'm not calling you because of my son; I'm calling you because I want to hear more about Jesus."

She invited me to a church where an atheist was ministering on how he found Jesus. She witnessed to me on the way to the church and again on the way home.

I drank a lot at that time and did drugs almost all the time. I am just thankful I never got strung out on them. When I got back to the house I had a lot on my mind. With a fifth of Jim Bean in hand I went to my bedroom and shut the door. I knelt down by my bed and prayed a simple prayer.

"Lord if it's true what she said about you coming into my heart and being my Savior come into my heart now and save me. At that moment I felt this peace and this presence and this joy come over me when I prayed that I had never felt before.

After I accepted Christ into my heart I got up off my knees, walked straight into the kitchen and poured all the alcohol I had in the house down the drain. I did not have a desire for alcohol anymore. I was totally delivered and set free. I was just a fireball for God after that.

I still had suicidal thoughts. I did not understand that a demonic spirit followed me around. When things would get rough and I would have those thoughts I would say, "No devil."

I went through a program called Cleaning Stream and they cast a spirit of death out of my life and it manifested and left.

That same demon still comes around and says things like, "You'd be better off if you were with Christ now." I recognize where it comes from. Now it is more of a suggestion. Before it was a strong desire to do it.

"I learned Jesus was the way out."

I learned Jesus was the way out. Jesus brings life. He gave me life. The enemy is about killing, stealing, and destroying. If you wonder if God is there, ask Him and He will reveal Himself to you. He will give you hope and He will give you a way out. Anything else is straight from hell.

If you are having strong desires to take your life know that it is not you and to get relief will take you getting the spirit of death out of your life. It is not your own thoughts. It is a demon. I wish I had known this. Now you do.

I encourage you if you are struggling in this area to cry out to God. If you have accepted Christ already you have rights and privileges as a child of God. You can get rid of the voices of the demons (that sound like your thoughts) through Christ by telling them to stop in the name of Jesus. And then seek help from someone you know who has Jesus in their life that can help you and counsel you.

You can also pray this prayer in the meantime:

Father, in the name of Jesus I cry out to you and ask You to come into my life. I ask you to reveal yourself to me. I ask that the price that Jesus paid by shedding his blood on the cross for me, would cover my entire life, my sins, my past, and my future. Forgive me for everything I have ever done wrong. Give me a new life, a fresh start, a second chance. Give me relief and healing from the pain in my soul. Heal my inner wounds and make me whole. And deliver me out of all the destructive forces in my life. Amen.

Chapter Insights

I know this woman personally. I have known her for many years. I would have never known the anguish and the agony she endured because of her abuse.

Kim has a strong spiritual impact on all those around her. She is determined to live her life to the fullest. I think in one way once you have faced death it gives you an appreciation for life and for second chances that would never be there otherwise.

"Abuse does not have an age, a color or a nationality attached to it."

Kim's story of abuse in her childhood is echoed in the hearts of many young children, both male and female.

Abuse does not have an age, a color or a nationality attached to it. Abuse is everywhere and it can often occur in the least likely families. Poverty is not an indication of abuse. Rich people have abuse in their families too.

"Here are some things healthy families do."

There are several ways you can determine if your family is functional and healthy or dysfunctional and unhealthy. Here are some things healthy families do. They love one another, they laugh together, they support one another, they are kind and patient, they have healthy boundaries and they encourage independence. They have a positive attitude, accept one another's faults and ideas, and they are nurturing.

"Here are some things unhealthy families or relationships do."

If your family or if your relationship is dysfunctional or unhealthy you will see things like disrespect. Here are some things unhealthy families or relationships do. There will be feelings of fear that include the fear of abandonment, the fear of losing control, the fear of what will happen next. Poor self-care is involved, low self-esteem and self-confidence as well as being harsh, critical of others and yourself, and a focus on the other person's problems. Jealousy, excuses, threats, intimidation, blame, violence, mistreatment, and a lack of friends are all dangerous signs that you are in an abusive or unhealthy relationship.

I encourage you to tell your story to others and encourage them. Impart hope to someone else who may be struggling like you did. Your testimony can and will impact others for the glory of God.

You can take what the enemy of your soul was using to

destroy you and help others with it. You can turn what was meant to harm you and use it for the good of others. Make the enemy pay for what he did to you by telling others how you overcame and are now on the other side. Tell them how you are living in victory now.

12

DON'T GIVE UP,
THERE STILL IS HOPE!
author chooses to stay anonymous
This testimony is unedited and quoted as it was written

Hi I'm a 15-year-old girl and was very suicidal nearly the whole last year but I got over it and I want to tell my story to help those people who feel like I did some time ago.

It all started at primary school with some guys in my class bullying me. The bullying went on for almost 10 years in every class and school I went to because some of that bullies always where in the same class. Over that long time I became very insecure and also depressed. Depression really started when I was 12 or 13 and I started cutting and burning myself when I was 14.

But suicidal thoughts came earlier than self-harming. They were one of the first things make me notice that I'm really depressed. It was in Easter holidays when I first hold a knife in my hand considering to kill myself. These thoughts accompanied me for the next month till I couldn't cope it anymore and started hurting myself.

Actually it wasn't really the first time I hurt myself (when I was in primary school I sometimes bit my lip or finger, pulled out my hair or knocked my head against a wall to deal with the mental pain the bullying caused) but it was the first time I saw my own blood when I hurt myself and the first time I did it totally on purpose.

In this time I wasn't able to walk to school (though bullying has stopped 3 or 4 months ago) or meet with the few friends I had without thinking about suicide. I couldn't look at trains, knifes, scissors, bridges and so on without wanting to hurt or kill myself. My friends knew about it and once I sent a suicide note to them. Well, they wanted to help me and I really am thankful for that but that wasn't the point that saved me nor the psychotherapist I went to since April 2014.

It was two other points that changed my life completely even though they don't seem very powerful on first sight:

First thing is not a thing but a person namely my little brother. He's 11-years-old and I really like him because he's so similar and close to me, I can talk about everything with him. He's very sensitive and insecure sometimes and I feared that he would be very depressed about my suicide. He was the only person I really felt close to during my depression, the most other people I liked but not felt close to because I felt so numb.

> *"…both the scars on my skin and the ones on my soul were nearly healed"*

Second thing was that bullying has stopped months before.

Actually there was no good reason for me to be depressed anymore. Anyway I WAS depressed but some day in December or January I suddenly kind of woke up from the nightmare I was in for years. I realized my life wasn't as bad as I thought and that both the scars on my skin and the ones on my soul were nearly healed and that I wasn't that numb anymore. So I decided to help others who suffer the way I did and that gives me the strength to live on.

So now I'm happy even though I did not have a proper childhood which results in me behaving and feeling like a child most of the time. But I overcame my bullying trauma, my depressions and suicidal thoughts and got the chance to start a new life.

"Most suicides are committed on impulse."

Actually in the vast majority of cases suicide is preventable. If you feel like killing yourself please first stop for a moment. Say to yourself you could also wait for three or more days until you are going to commit suicide. Most suicides are committed on impulse. So if you wait some days you may still not feel good but you maybe wouldn't make the same decision again. Many people who tried to kill there selves but didn't succeed regret their suicide attempt.

Now try to think about something good and if that isn't possible for you in that moment try at least to find some things that aren't bad. Search for something you would possibly miss when you're dead or someone who means much to you and you think wouldn't be able to manage your death. And trust me these things and people exist, for you as well as for me and for every person on this world. Even if you don't see them NOW, they ARE there and one day you will be able to see them, one day you'll be able to smile and be happy again.

But if you leave now, you will never be able to experience that WONDERFUL day. Wouldn't that be very sad? So don't take away this great chance of a better life by a hasty action. Think well, I'm sure you CAN find something good in life if you search close enough. And let me tell you another thing you should NEVER EVER forget: YOU, yes you, I mean you sitting there with sad eyes on the edge with no hope anymore, YOU, my friend, YOU ARE WORTH LIVING!!!

There is always a reason to keep on walking and fighting and searching. And YOU are able to find it and in any case you're worth it because YOU'RE PRECIOUS AND IRREPLACEABLE, YOU'RE UNIQUE AND WONDERFUL AND IMPORTANT.

And now allow yourself a SMILE and make yourself a nice day. Do something you like and don't worry. I guarantee EVERYTHING WILL BE OK ONE DAY.

Chapter Insights

Out of the mouths of babes. This young 15 year old certainly speaks from her heart to yours. I hope you are hearing what she is saying. She speaks from experience. She speaks from her personal place of pain. She speaks encouragement and hope to you from her understanding.

How did this young one get so wise in just 15 years of living?

She shared about the scars on her skin and her soul. I know many of you reading this book have some very deep internal wounds. I am not negating them in this book, but

I am saying again that healing is possible.

"Don't let your wounds ruin your life."

This young woman is telling you not to give up. There is still hope to be found. Look for it. Don't let your wounds ruin your life. Find help. Look at the back of the book under resources to find places you can call or websites you can visit.

She said most suicides are committed "on impulse" and that is true from the research I have done. Including my son, remember he said he wasn't thinking about killing his self, he just saw the knife and started cutting. How many people have just decided to get the gun, take the pill, jump from the building, get the knife, drive the car into a tree, etc. at that very moment?

"spirit of suicide"

I want to share with you a testimony I have with a "spirit of suicide" and yes I said a spirit of suicide.

"There are, it may be, so many kinds of voices in the world, and none of them is without signification." 1 Cor. 14:10

I was driving down the road, a four lane highway to be exact. I pulled into the turnaround median and two 18 wheelers were coming towards me. The spirit of suicide spoke to me, in my head, and said, "Why don't you pull out in from of them. If one doesn't kill you the other one will."

There was no part of me that was suicidal. I was not depressed. I was happy. I am usually always a happy person. Why that spirit would say that to me had nothing to do with an internal wound. It was there to harass me and perhaps even get rid of me.

I simply laughed, recognizing it for what it was, and said, "Shut up!. I have no intention of killing myself now or ever." I have not heard anything from that spirit since that day.

That was not the first time I had that spirit speak thoughts into my head. All they can do is plant ideas. They cannot make you entertain the ideas or thoughts. You are the one in control. Not them.

I understand that talking about spirits might be a little unusual or weird for you. Let me tell you though that they are real. If you think about your thoughts for a few minutes you will be able to distinguish between your thoughts and those of the enemy who wants to destroy you, keep you depressed, and full of pain, so you do not fulfill your destiny and live a full and abundant life.

"Why be the victim of an unseen negative force?"

Remember we talked about spirits in chapter 1. The more you learn about the spiritual world you live in the better off you will be. Why be the victim of an unseen negative force? Stand up and fight the enemy, the negative in your life, the depression, and the voices you hear in your head telling you to kill yourself or to hurt yourself.

Oh yes, I have heard them, "You might as well just kill yourself. No one loves you. You will never be good enough." And on and on and on. For years I was tormented by thoughts but I was never really taking any of them seriously. I knew there was more to life than what I had and I truly wanted to live. I did not want to die.

Hearing voices in your head does not mean you are crazy. It means you are normal. Well, at least normal if you are hearing about three to four voices. If you are hearing more than a few voices in your head you need to seek some professional help and sort through them. Sometimes those voices are a result of severe recurrent and prolonged traumatic events in a person's life. Sometimes this causes the soul to split to protect itself.

Remember I am not a licensed professional, but I am a professional in my field of spiritual counseling and I have worked with many people who have been shattered by a traumatic lifestyle. Some were ritually satanically abused in a cult, some had multiple personalities, some were involved in a cult and needed to be deprogrammed, but all of them had two things in common: more than one voice in their heads and severe trauma in their lives.

"We all hear our own voice."

Let me share with you about the voices in our heads. We all hear our own voice. Our voice sounds like us. It is us. Our real self. The I part of us. Our thoughts consist of thoughts like this, "I am hungry. I want some ice cream. I am going to … I want… I will… I am… they are always focused on me because It really is all about me/I.

"We are all in a personal war with the voice of the enemy."

The voice of the enemy is always accusing, always negative, always condemning and making you feel guilty and ashamed, less than and totally unworthy. The voice of the enemy uses "you" statements. "You are stupid." And eventually you believe the lie and start saying "I am so stupid!" when you do something wrong. Same thing with statements like "I am so ugly." "No one will ever want me." I think you get the idea. Negative, and hurtful, insulting and degrading, and causes strife and division. This is what makes us gossip, backbite, accuse others, and it is what makes us so hard on ourselves. We are all in a personal war with the voice of the enemy.

"My sheep hear my voice"

Then we have the third voice we should be hearing, and do hear when we recognize it: The voice of God. His voice can be that still quiet voice that leads you if you are His.

> "...the sheep hear his voice: and he calleth his own sheep by name, and leadeth them out. John 10:3 KJV

> My sheep hear my voice, and I know them, and they follow me: John 10:27 KJV

Here are some additional Truths about hearing God's voice from the King James Version Bible.

> Blessed is the man that walketh not in the counsel of the ungodly, nor standeth in the way of sinners, nor sitteth in the seat of the scornful. (The ungodly have a voice which leads the sinner. This is their own spirit, the spirit of flesh or the spirit of the devil) Psalm 1:1

When I hear the voice of the Lord it is sometimes just an inner nudging, a feeling, an image, a sound, a word (that I will usually have to look up in the dictionary - even with a master's degree), literally, internally or externally. He has spoken to me verbally before when He said, "This is the man you are going to marry and spend the rest of your life with." It scared me actually. I turned and looked around to see who said that. Of course I did not see Him but I felt His powerful presence. Didn't the Scripture say He leads the sheep?

His voice is more of a command. For example, when I am driving, sometimes I will forget to put my seatbelt on and I will hear this voice say, "Put your seatbelt on." Or sometimes when I get all caught up in worship while I am driving I will hear, "Slow down." And as soon as I hear and obey I will see the police or Highway Patrol and I am saved from getting a ticket.

"God's voice protects us."

Am I saying we do not have to obey the law? Heaven forbid. I am saying we are human and we forget things, or we get distracted and our mind is on something else which can cause us to unintentionally break the law. Not out of rebellion, but out of distraction or carelessness. I am thankful for the thousands of dollars I have saved over the past 20 years in tickets!

God's voice protects us. I was driving down the highway 70 miles an hour and hear this voice say, "Pull over at Dairy Queen." I argued with the voice. I did not know it was the Lord speaking to me. I heard it again. Again I argued, "I am not hungry." And again I heard it and again I said, "But I am not thirsty." Finally the voice was no longer soft and suggesting it was commanding and louder, with a sense of urgency.

I knew I had to obey the voice, which I finally figured out was the Lord. When I turned into the driveway the front driver's side tire and wheel fell off causing the four-wheel-drive Blazer to crash to the pavement. The front end of the driver's side of the vehicle crashed about 2 feet to the ground, causing me to jerk to a complete stop. Guess what was right next to me? A tire shop! This is how the Lord will work in your life too.

"Without His voice life is dark and without hope."

What would have happened had I not heeded that voice and obeyed? You would not be reading this book right now would you? This is only one of many times I have heard the voice of the Lord or an angel which is a messenger of the Lord.

There are so many stories I could share, but the point is that God's voice is one that we were created to hear. He is the one who encourages you, comforts you, strengthens you, and loves you. Without His voice life is dark and without hope.

"Lord what do you think of me?"

Prepare to hear the voice of your Creator. Get a piece of paper and a pen, sit quietly somewhere and ask Him, "Lord what do You think of me?" Then just be still. Just wait patiently. Whatever you hear, write it down.

I was teaching a class once to do this and decided to do it with them again. I was so surprised by what the Lord spoke to me that it transformed my relationship with Him forever.

He said, "You know when you have your first child and you look at that precious face for the first time; and that feeling of awe, excitement, and amazement all at the same time? That's how I feel about you all the time."

How can hearing something like that not change your life? Big tears streamed down my face. He was not finished. He was determined to describe to me just how much He loved me in terms I could not mistake or ever forget.

Then He spoke and said, "You know when you fall in love? You cannot stop thinking about them, you talk about them all the time, they are the first thing on your mind when you wake up and the last thing on your mind when you go to sleep, and you want to spend every waking moment with the one you love? That's how I fell about you all the time.

More tears streamed down my face. I was a woman undone. I had never heard such beautiful words, such encouraging and loving words before in my life.

But wait, there's more. He then said, "You know how much you love your poodle? How when you leave and you come back, it does not matter if you just walked out the door and right back in, or if you have been gone for hours, the excitement he has to see you is equally the same. He dances around and rejoices over your return. That's how I feel about you. I rejoice when you come home to spend time with Me."

By this time I have used multiple Kleenex. My heart is filled to overflowing. I feel the love of My Heavenly Father in a way that I had never imagined possible. So can you. Simply take the time to talk to Him, or pray, or just be still before Him, it does not matter what you call it. Just wait for His reply. It will come. Pray, seek answers to your questions, and then listen. Be prepared to hear. Expect to hear what He says. Write it down. It will change your life.

13

PROTECTING OURSELVES
author chooses to remain anonymous
This testimony is unedited and quoted as it was written

I am feeling low. I called my crisis line THREE times before I got it out what was really bothering me. I finally admitted how I don't want to be, that I was looking for the pills I knew would work. :((((but I could not find them. I stopped looking, good or bad…

The thing is, isn't it crazy to be mad at the world and people around you but then, you take it out on yourself??

I mean, really, the reaction of wanting to hurt yourself because the world seems off kilter, that is crazy!

And yet, here I am, once again…   (Still, something to think about, help us resist and rethink…)

"Depression is turning on ourselves"

P.S... the more I think of this, the more I realize it's true. Depression is turning on ourselves, harming us because there are situations that either are out of our control or seem so.

But think of it... when there is something wrong (right or wrong in our thinking) our reaction is to hurt ourselves- by our words or deeds, thoughts or reactions. The pain protects us from the deeper pain we are ignoring/ running away from.

But isn't this the case of the cure is worse than the problem? If you truly think about it, it is so.

"Maybe we have to protect ourselves"

Maybe we have to protect ourselves, when we have pain and start to "punish" ourselves (words, thoughts, emotions, deeds, etc.), see a "stop sign" in our mind and replace that with a sign that says "KIND to me".

"Protecting ourselves should be our number one priority"

It may not do a lot for whatever is happening that hurts so much. But protecting ourselves should be our number one priority.

Chapter Insights

I want you to know from this testimony that it does not matter how many time you reach out for help for the same thing. You just keep reaching out until you find and get the help you need. Help is there. Find it.

The point this author made about how we get angry at others but take it out on ourselves is true. It is backwards but true. Why would you punish yourself for something someone else did? Does it even make any sense to do that? Of course not, but yet this is the reality for many. As if hurting ourselves is somehow going to make the other person suffer for what they did. Even if it did make them suffer even a little is it really worth it?

The one who wrote this chapter's testimony was figuring something out. That something is called balance. They were realizing the need to find harmony within regardless of the situation or the circumstances. We cannot always be in control of our own lives. We rarely have control if the truth be told. There is usually always someone else in control of our time, our finances, our future, etc.

The sooner we can learn to let go and let God have control of our lives the sooner we can walk in peace. God created you with a plan in place. Not that we do not get to make decisions and not that we do not have a choice in things, but the overall blessings and the overall direction for your life was established so that you could live your best life ever.

We fall short of the best that God has for us when we sin, when we rebel against Him and His way of doing things. We miss the mark. We tie the hands of the Lord when He tries to bless us and force Him, if you will, to withhold our blessings and our provision. That is also our choice. It is something we are in control of.

There is a quote from Marcus Aurelius Meditations: The Stoic Ideal that states what I am trying to say in a much better way:

> "The only things that matter to a wise and philosophic individual are the things completely under your control. You can't control the movement of the sun and the planets, you can't control whether a leaky ship sinks or makes it to port. You can't control the weather, you can't control other people, and you can't control the society around you. There is only one thing and one thing only

that you are in control of: that is you. Your will, your intentions, yourself. The wise man is the person entirely in control of his own soul. Who takes utter and complete responsibility of his actions and is indifferent to everything else." Michael Sugrue

There are some things in life you can control. Lori Deschene has written an article: Here are 50 Things You Can Control Right Now. I have chosen a few of them to share with you so that you know beyond a shadow of a doubt that there are many things in your life that you can control.

You can control:
1. When you ask for help.
2. How you act on your feelings.
3. How you interpret situations.
4. How nice you are to yourself in your head.
5. Whether you think positive or negative thoughts.
6. How much time you spend worrying.
7. How often you think about your past.
8. Whether or not you communicate something that's on your mind.
9. How many risks you take.
10. How creative/innovative you are in your thinking.
11. How many times you say "I love you."

There are many other things in your life you can begin to control. How you feel about yourself is certainly one of them. Start taking the negative and self-destructive thoughts and realizing they are not the truth. Then find the truth based on who God says you are. After all, doesn't it make sense that the ONE WHO created you, knows the number of every hair on your head, who thinks about you more than there are grains of sand on the shores and in the deserts, the ONE WHO knows your thoughts before you even say them, and the ONE WHO knit you together in your mother's womb not only intimately knows you but also wants the very best for you? Of course He does.

"Light can shine in your life and change things for you in an instant"

I challenge you now as I close out this last chapter to begin making the changes in your life you need to make. Take one small step in the opposite direction you were headed in. If you are planning your suicide even after reading this book my prayer is that you will realize that you are valuable and that even as dark and depressing as things may seem right now, the Light can shine in your life and change things for you in an instant.

You have read testimonies of those who have tried and failed and are so glad they did. You have also read the reality of those who have tried and did and the devastating emotions and years of grief the loved ones, and you have more of them than you think you do, you will leave behind.

Please understand you are not alone. You are never alone. Help is a prayer away. It does not matter what you say in that prayer as long as you call upon the name of Jesus. Let me give you a pattern of a prayer you might say:

Father, in the name of Jesus,

I cry out to You today, right here, right now. I need You and I need help.

Come save me from this life of pain and despair; pull me up out of this pit of agony and depression. Bring peace and healing to my body, mind, soul, and spirit. Heal my body from all the abuse it has endured either at the hands of others or of my own doing.

Renew my mind. Heal my broken heart. Heal my wounded soul. Put a right spirit within me. Reveal to me the depth, and the height, and the width of great Your love for me.

I forgive You Lord for the times I have blamed my circumstances on You. I forgive others for hurting me, using me, abusing me, neglecting me, rejecting me, and everything else they have ever done. I want to forgive so I can be forgiven. I ask You to forgive me as I have sinned against You, others, and myself. Father, I forgive myself for everything I have done against myself. I choose love. I choose to walk the higher road and the better path.

Thank You Father for translating me (taking me from one place to the other) out of the kingdom of darkness and into the Kingdom of Light. Thank You Father that when I call upon You, You are hearing me, listening to me, and answering me. Thank You for saving me and healing me. Thank You for showing me the Love I have always looked for and needed.

Help me live for You now. Teach me Your ways. Guide me in the direction You want me to go in. Bless me now as I turn from all my unhealthy ways and establish new thinking patterns, new habits, and new truths about myself.

Thank You Father for all You have done for me. Amen

BIBLIOGRAPHY

Ariii. (2015). I'm glad I failed. Retrieved July 13, 2015 from
http://suicideproject.org/2015/06/337264/

Chambers, M., Liu, M., and Moore, C., (2012). Drunk Driving
by the Numbers. Retrieved on Jun3 26, 2015 from
http://www.rita.dot.gov/bts/sites/rita.dot.gov.bts/files/p
ublications/by_the_numbers/drunk_driving/index.html

Deschene, L., (2013). 50 Things You Can Control Right Now.
Retrieved on October 25, 2015 from
http://tinybuddha.com/blog/50-things-you-can-control-
right-now/

Lonely Days. [Picture]. (n.d.). Retrieved on November 03,
2015 from
http://services.flikie.com/view/v3/android/wallpapers/3
3563419.

López De Victoria, S. (2014). How to Spot a Narcissist. *Psych
Central.* Retrieved on November 3, 2015, from
http://psychcentral.com/blog/archives/2008/08/04/ho

w-to-spot-a-narcissist/

Myss, C. (2011). *Healing from soul wounds.* Retrieved on July 25, 2015 from https://scripturalteachings.wordpress.com/2011/06/13/healing-from-spiritual-wounds/

Shain, M. (1985). Hearts that broke long ago. Bantam Books, Inc., New York, NY.

United States Department of Traffic Safety Facts (USTDSO). (2009). Pedestrians 2009 data. Retrieved on June 26, 2015 from http://www-nrd.nhtsa.dot.gov/Pubs/811394.pdf.

RESOURCES

24 Hour Addiction Helpline: 888-327-5040

Alcohol Anonymous: http://www.aa.org/

Alliance of Hope for Suicide Survivors
http://www.allianceofhope.org/

American Psychiatric Association
1-888-357-7924

American Psychological Association
1-800-374-2721
Provides referrals to licensed psychologists.

Celebrate Recovery
http://www.celebraterecovery.com/cr-groups/group-locator

Centre for Suicide Prevention
(403) 245-3900

HEARTBEAT: Grief Support Following Suicide

1-800-SUICIDE
http://heartbeatsurvivorsaftersuicide.org/

International Association for Suicide Prevention
+33-562-29-19 47

National Center on Elder Abuse, Administration on Aging 1-800-677-1116
http://www.ncea.aoa.gov or call

National Suicide Prevention Lifeline
1-800-273-TALK (8255)

Suicide Awareness Voices of Education
(952) 946-7998
http://www.save.org/

Suicide Prevention Resource Center
1-877-GET-SPRC
suicidepreventionlifeline.org

Youth Suicide Prevention Program
http://www.yspp.org

ABOUT THE AUTHOR

Cindy Hyde, MA is passionate about helping people. She is an Ordained Minister, Author, Speaker, Teacher, Pastoral Counselor, Professional Life Coach, and CEO/Founder of The East Texas Healing Center in Nacogdoches, TX where she and her husband Michael live. They have four children, (two are married), 11 grandchildren, one great-granddaughter, and their four-legged fur-baby named Quincy.

Visit www.cindyhyde.com for more info.

CONTACT THE AUTHOR

Cindy Hyde's mailing address is:

> 407 E. Hospital St.
> Nacogdoches, TX 75961
>
> Website: www.cindyhyde.com
>
> Cell Phone: 936-615-1497
>
> Email: cindylhyde@gmail.com
>
> **East Texas Healing Center**
> Easttexashealingcenter.org
> Office Phone: 936-569-7729

Cindy is available to minister at your church, home group, Sunday School group, ministry, conference or school.

OTHER BOOKS BY THE AUTHOR

Making Peace With Your Past:
One Choice at a Time (Available on Amazon.com)

A Woman of Acts

Prisoners of War Shackled No More

Flames of Change

Wisdoms from My Heart

Beyond Abuse: A Journey of Restoration